BIG IDEAS
MATH.
Algebra 2

Assessment Book

- Prerequisite Skills Test

- Pre-Course Test with Item Analysis

- Quiz

- Chapter Tests

- Alternative Assessment

- Performance Task

- Quarterly Standards Based Test

- Post Course Test with Item Analysis

Erie, Pennsylvania

Photo Credits

Cover Image CVADRAT/Shutterstock.com

Big Ideas Learning and *Big Ideas Math* are registered trademarks of Larson Texts, Inc.

ISBN 13: 978-1-60840-857-3
ISBN 10: 1-60840-857-4

123456789-VLP-18 17 16 15 14

Contents

About the Assessment Book

Prerequisite Skills Test with Item Analysis

The Prerequisite Skills Test checks students' understanding of previously learned mathematical skills they will need to be successful in Algebra 2. The Item Analysis can be used to determine topics that need to be reviewed.

Pre-Course Test with Item Analysis
Post Course Test with Item Analysis

The Pre-Course Test and Post Course Test cover key concepts that students will learn in their Algebra 2 course. The Item Analysis can be used to determine topics that need to be reviewed.

Quiz

The Quiz provides ongoing assessment of student understanding. The quiz appears at the halfway point of the chapter.

Chapter Tests

The Chapter Tests provide assessment of student understanding of key concepts taught in the chapter. There are two tests for each chapter.

Alternative Assessment with Scoring Rubric

Each Alternative Assessment includes at least one multi-step problem that combines a variety of concepts from the chapter. Students are asked to explain their solutions, write about the mathematics, or compare and analyze different situations.

Performance Task

The Performance Task presents an assessment in a real-world situation. Every chapter has a task that allows students to work with multiple standards and apply their knowledge to realistic scenarios.

Quarterly Standards Based Test

The Quarterly Standards Based Test provides students practice answering questions in standardized test format. The assessments are cumulative and cover material from multiple chapters of the textbook. The questions represent problem types and reasoning patterns frequently found on standardized tests.

Name _____ Date _____

In Exercises 1–5, solve the equation for x.   *Answers*

1. $3x^2 = 9$ 2. $4x + 5 = -3$
                                                                1. _____

3. $5x + 7 = 3x + 15$ 4. $3(x + 2) = 2(10 - x) + 11$
                                                                2. _____

5. $|3x + 4| = 8$ 3. _____

                                                                4. _____

6. The shape of a dome can be modeled by the equation $h = -2d^2 + 100$
   where h is the height (in feet) of the dome from the floor d feet from its center.   5. _____
   How far from the center of the dome is the height 50 feet?
                                                                6. _____

7. Simplify using the order of operations: $(3 + 2)^3 - 5 \times 6 - \frac{9}{3}$.   7. _____

                                                                8. _____

8. A cab charges $0.10 per mile and a flat fee of $3.00. Write an equation to
   model the price y of an x-mile-long cab ride.
                                                                9. _____

9. Use the discriminate to determine the number of solutions to the quadratic
   equation $y = 3x^2 - 4x + 6$.   10. ___See left.___

                                                                11. ___See left.___

In Exercises 10–12, graph the equation, inequality, or system of inequalities.
                                                                12. ___See left.___

10. $y = -3x + 2$ 11. $y < -3|x + 1|$

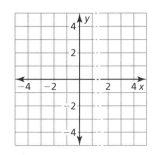   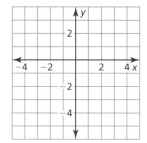

12. $y > 2x - 5$

   $y \geq -\frac{1}{2}x + 2$

Name_____ Date_____

Skills Test
Prerequisite Skills Test (continued)

13. If $f(x) = 7x^2 + 5$, compute $f(3)$.

14. On a certain day there was a near constant snowfall rate of 0.50 inch per hour. After 4 hours there were 10 inches of snow on the ground (including some from the day before). Write an equation that models the amount of snowfall in inches y after x hours.

15. You are traveling away from home at a constant speed. After 3 hours you are 60 miles from home and after 7 hours you are 160 miles from home. Write an equation that models y, your distance (in miles) from home after x hours.

16. Write an equation representing the translation of $f(x) = 7x + 3$ down 4 units.

17. The average attendance of a certain fitness class that meets daily for the first 4 days are given: 4, 10, 16, and 22. Write a formula for the general term a_n which models the pattern.

In Exercises 18–20, solve the system using any method.

18. $y = 3x + 2$
$y = 7x - 10$

19. $3x + 2y = 8$
$y = 3x + 1$

20. $2x + 2y = 8$
$3x + y = 10$

21. Simplify $(3x^2)^5$.

22. Simplify $\dfrac{3x^4y^2}{18x^2y^7}$.

Answers

13. _____
14. _____
15. _____
16. _____
17. _____
18. _____
19. _____
20. _____
21. _____
22. _____

Copyright © Big Ideas Learning, LLC
All rights reserved.

Algebra 2
Assessment Book

3

Name _____ Date _____

In Exercises 23 and 24, use the two-way table that shows the results of a
blood test used to detect a certain disease for a sample of patients.

Answers

	Positive Result	Negative Result
Disease Present	103	15
Disease Not Present	17	207

23. Determine the probability that the blood test will detect the disease, if you
    have the disease.

24. What is the probability that you have the disease, if your blood test reports a
    positive result?

25. The selling price of a certain collector's item was $10 in 2000 and $15 in
    2001. If the selling price of the item follows a geometric sequence, what
    would the price of the item be in 2002?

26. The population of a certain city grows exponentially. When the city was
    founded, it only had 1000 residents. After 1 year the city had 1050 residents.
    Write an equation that models the population y of the city after x years.

27. Graph the equation $y = (x + 2)^2 + 5$.

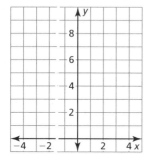

In Exercises 28 and 29, use the scores for a physics test: 95, 90, 88, 75, 70, 92.

28. Find the mean of the scores.

29. What is the standard deviation of the scores?

30. Simplify $(3x^2 + 5x + 7) - (3x + 5x^2)$.

31. Simplify $(x + 1)(x^2 - x + 1)$.

32. Solve $\begin{array}{l} x^2 + y = 7 \\ 3x + y = 9 \end{array}$ for x and y.

23. _____

24. _____

25. _____

26. _____

27. ___See left.___

28. _____

29. _____

30. _____

31. _____

32. _____

4 **Algebra 2**
Assessment Book

Name_____ Date_____

Answers

33. The length of the base of a certain rectangle is modeled by the equation

    $b = \sqrt{\dfrac{A}{5}}$ where b is the length of the base and A is the area of the rectangle.

    If the base of the rectangle is 8 inches, what is the area of the rectangle?

34. Simplify $x^{1/5} + y^{5/3}$ using radicals and integer exponents.

35. Solve $0 = (x + 2)^2 - 25$.

36. Solve $3x^2 + 5x - 12 = 0$.

37. A rectangular yard has a length that is 7 feet longer than its width. If the
    perimeter of the yard is 46 feet, what is the area of the yard?

38. Graph $y = |2x + 1|$.

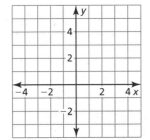

39. Write an equation of the line.

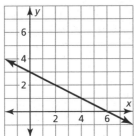

40. Consider the inequality $6 < |5x - 1|$.

    a. Solve for x.

    b. Graph the solution on the number line.

33. _____

34. _____

35. _____

36. _____

37. _____

38. __See left.__

39. _____

40. a._____

    b.__See left.__

Item Number	Skills	Item Number	Skills
1	solving quadratic equations by using square roots	19	solving systems of equations by substitution
2	solving two step linear equations	20	solving systems of equations by elimination
3	solving linear equations with variables on both sides	21	simplifying using the properties of exponents
4	solving linear equations requiring distribution	22	simplifying rational expressions
5	solving absolute value equations	23	computing probability using two-way tables
6	solving quadratic equations	24	computing probability using two-way tables
7	simplifying with order of operations	25	modeling with geometric sequences
8	modeling with linear equations	26	modeling exponential growth
9	using the discriminate	27	graphing quadratic functions
10	graphing linear equations	28	computing the measure of center of data
11	graphing absolute value inequalities	29	computing the measure of variation of data
12	graphing systems of inequalities	30	subtracting polynomial expressions
13	evaluating functions	31	multiplying polynomial expressions
14	modeling with linear equations	32	solving nonlinear systems of equations
15	modeling with linear equations	33	solving radical equations
16	transforming linear functions	34	simplifying using properties of rational exponents
17	modeling arithmetic sequences	35	solving quadratic equations
18	solving systems of equations by substitution	36	solving quadratic equations

Item Number	Skills
37	modeling with algebraic expressions
38	graphing absolute value equations

Item Number	Skills
39	writing linear equations
40	solving absolute value inequalities

Name _____ Date _____

Perform the operation.

Answers

1. $\dfrac{x+2}{x^2-9} \div \dfrac{x^2+4x+4}{x^2+6x+9}$

2. $\dfrac{3}{x+2} + \dfrac{x}{x-3}$

3. A ladder leans against a house making a $30°$ angle with the ground. If the ladder touches the house at a point 10 feet high, how long is the ladder?

4. After 3 weeks, a plant is 8 centimeters tall. After 4 weeks, it has grown to 10 centimeters. If the plant grows following an arithmetic sequence, how tall will it be after 25 weeks?

Describe the transformation of the graph of $g(x)$ represented by the equation of $f(x)$.

5. $f(x) = 2|x-1|$ and $g(x) = |x|$

6. $f(x) = (x+3)^2 - 4$ and $g(x) = x^2$

7. $f(x) = 3x^3 + 3x + 4$ and $g(x) = x^3 + x$

8. $f(x) = -3^{-x}$ and $g(x) = 3^x$

9. You start off the day owing \$5 to a friend. After 3 hours of work at x dollars per hour, you pay the debt to your friend and have \$4 remaining. Write an equation to model this situation.

10. Solve the system of equations.

$$4x + y = -3$$
$$5x + 3y = 12$$

11. The area of a rectangle can be modeled by $A = b(4-b)$, where A is the area of the rectangle and b is the length of the base (in inches). What is the greatest possible area of the rectangle?

12. Factor $x^2 + 7x + 12$.

13. The path of a soccer ball can be modeled by $h = -16t^2 + 12t + 3$, where h represents the height (in feet) of the ball after t seconds. At what time will the ball reach the ground? Round your answer to the nearest hundredth.

14. Convert $y = x^2 + 8x$ to vertex form.

1. _____
2. _____
3. _____
4. _____
5. _____
6. _____
7. _____
8. _____
9. _____
10. _____
11. _____
12. _____
13. _____
14. _____

Pre-Course **Pre-Course Test** (continued)

15. Solve the system of equations.

$$y = 3x^2$$
$$y = 5x + 2$$

16. Each test for a class was worth twice as many points as the previous test. If the first test was worth 6 points, what equation models the number of points the nth test is worth?

17. Solve $10 = 9x^2 - 134$ for x.

18. Graph $y > 3x^2 + 2$.

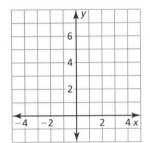

19. A company's minimum cost of $1000 occurs when operating for 16 hours per day. The cost of operating 8 hours per day would be $2600. If the company's costs can be modeled by a quadratic equation, write the equation which models the company's costs.

20. What are the first five terms of the geometric sequence $a_n = 3(2)^{n-1}$?

21. What are the first five terms of the following sequence $a_1 = 5$ and $a_n = a_{n-1} + 2n$?

22. Graph $y = x^3 + 2x + 2$.

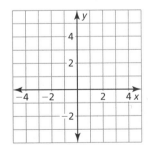

23. Simplify $\dfrac{x^4 - 16}{x^3 + 2x^2 + 4x + 8}$.

Answers

15._____

16._____

17._____

18.___See left.___

19._____

20._____

21._____

22.___See left.___

23._____

Pre-Course **Pre-Course Test** (continued)

24. Solve $x^4 + 6x^3 + 3x^2 - 10x = 0$ for x.

Answers

25. Write the polynomial of least degree which represents the graph.

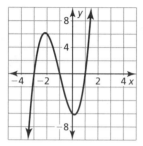

26. Simplify $\sqrt[3]{27x^9y^8}$ using rational exponents.

27. Graph $y = \dfrac{-3}{x + 2}$.

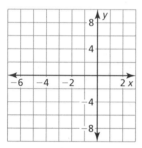

28. Let $f(x) = 3x + 6$ and $g(x) = 2x^2$. Find $f \bullet g$.

29. The rate you run to your friend's house is inversely proportional to the time it takes to get to the house. If it takes 30 minutes to get to the house when you run 7 miles per hour, find an equation relating the rate and time.

30. Solve $\dfrac{3}{x + 3} + \dfrac{2}{2x - 6} = \dfrac{7}{8}$ for x.

31. Solve $5^{3x} = 25^{x+2}$ for x.

32. Describe the transformation of the graph of $g(x) = \sin x$ represented by the equation $f(x) = \frac{1}{2} \sin x + 2$.

33. Simplify $\sin^2 x + \sin^2 x \cot^2 x$.

34. What is the probability of drawing a club or a jack from a standard 52 deck of cards?

24. _____

25. _____

26. _____

27. ___See left.___

28. _____

29. _____

30. _____

31. _____

32. _____

_____

33. _____

34. _____

10 **Algebra 2**
Assessment Book

Name_____ Date_____

Pre-Course **Pre-Course Test** (continued)

35. A bag contains three chocolate candies and two vanilla candies. What is the probability of drawing all three chocolate candies in three consecutive draws (without replacing them each time)?

36. How many two-letter code words can be made from the letters "MATH?"

37. The scores on a statistics test are normally distributed with a mean of 77 and a standard deviation of 3. What percent of students would you expect to score between 77 and 83?

38. Convert $\dfrac{5\pi}{6}$ to degrees.

39. What is the inverse of $f(x) = \sqrt{x + 2}$?

40. Compute $\log_4 5$ using the change-of-base formula.

41. Simplify $\left(x^2 + 5x + 5\right) - \left(2x^2 + 6\right)$.

42. Two students were chosen at random from each first period class and asked to complete a survey about their sleep habits. What sampling method was used?

43. The antenna of a parabolic dish is 20 meters above its vertex. What is an equation to represent the shape of the dish with vertex $(0, 0)$?

44. Consider the graph of the function.

    a. What is the domain of the function?

    b. What is the range of the function?

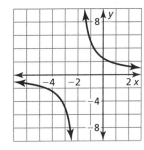

45. Simplify i^7.

46. Simplify $3i(2 - 5i)$.

47. Solve $x^2 + 5x - 2 < -8$ for x.

48. Evaluate the cosine of the angle of rotation which contains the point $(9, -3)$ on its terminal side.

Answers

35. _____

36. _____

37. _____

38. _____

39. _____

40. _____

41. _____

42. _____

43. _____

44. a._____

    b._____

45. _____

46. _____

47. _____

48. _____

Pre-Course Test Item Analysis

Item Number	Skills
1	dividing rational expressions
2	adding rational expressions
3	applying the right triangle trigonometry
4	modeling with arithmetic sequences
5	transforming absolute value functions
6	transforming quadratic functions
7	transforming polynomial functions
8	transforming exponential functions
9	modeling linear functions
10	solving systems of equations
11	identifying characteristics of quadratic functions
12	factoring polynomials
13	solving quadratic equations
14	completing the square
15	solving nonlinear systems of equations
16	modeling geometric sequences
17	solving quadratic equations
18	graphing quadratic inequalities in two variables
19	modeling with quadratic equations

Item Number	Skills
20	evaluating exponential functions
21	modeling with recursive sequences
22	graphing polynomial functions
23	dividing polynomials
24	solving polynomial equations
25	modeling with polynomial functions
26	simplifying using the properties of rational exponents
27	graphing rational functions
28	multiplying polynomial functions
29	modeling with inverse variation
30	solving rational equations
31	solving exponential equations
32	transforming trigonometric functions
33	simplifying using trigonometric functions
34	computing the probability of non-mutually exclusive events
35	computing the probability of dependent events
36	counting permutations
37	using normal distributions
38	converting between radians and degrees

Item Number	Skills
39	finding the inverse of a function
40	simplifying using the rules of logarithms
41	subtracting polynomial expressions
42	identifying sampling methods
43	translating between the geometric description and the equation of parabolas

Item Number	Skills
44	identifying the domain and range of a rational function
45	simplifying powers of i
46	multiplying complex numbers
47	solving quadratic inequalities
48	evaluating trigonometric ratios of any angle

Name _____ Date _____

Identify the function family to which _g_ belongs.

Answers

1. $g(x) = \dfrac{1}{5}x + 2$ **2.** $g(x) = 4x^2 - 6$ **3.** $g(x) = |x - 3| + 5$

1. _____

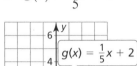

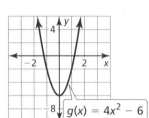

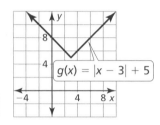

2. _____

3. _____

4. ___See left.___

Graph the function and its parent function. Then describe the transformation.

4. $f(x) = 5x$ **5.** $f(x) = 3(x + 2)^2$ **6.** $f(x) = -|x + 4| - 3$

5. ___See left.___

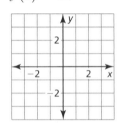

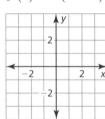

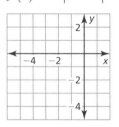

6. ___See left.___

Write a function _g_ whose graph represents the indicated transformation of the graph of _f_.

7. $f(x) = 4x + 1$; translation 2 units left

7. _____

8. $f(x) = -4|x - 2|$; vertical shrink by a factor of $\dfrac{1}{2}$

8. _____

9. Let _g_ be a translation 4 units down and a horizontal shrink by a factor of $\dfrac{1}{4}$ of the graph of $f(x) = x$.

9. _____

10. Let _g_ be a reflection in the _x_-axis and a vertical stretch by a factor of 3, followed by a translation 4 units down and 1 unit right of the graph of $f(x) = |x|$.

10. _____

11. _____

11. The total reimbursement (in dollars) for driving a company car _m_ miles can be modeled by the function $f(x) = 0.45m + 5$. After a policy change, five more dollars are added on and then the total reimbursement amount is multiplied by 1.25. Describe how to transform the graph of _f_. What is the total reimbursement for a trip of 95 miles?

Name_____ Date _____

Write an equation of the line and interpret the slope.

Answers

1.
    Child Growth Rate

2.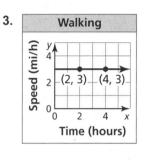
    Home Phone Sales

3. **Walking**

1. _____

_____

_____

_____

_____

2. _____

_____

_____

_____

_____

Solve the system. Check your solution, if possible.

4. $3x - 3y + z = 10$
    $3x + 2y - 3z = -2$
    $-3x + z = -2$

5. $3x + 5y + 4z = 13$
    $5x + 2y + 3z = -9$
    $6x + 3y + 4z = -8$

6. $-x - y - 2z = 9$
    $-2x + 2y - 2z = -8$
    $x - y + z = 5$

7. $x + y + z = 9$
    $2x - 3y + 4z = 7$
    $x - 4y + 3z = -2$

3. _____

_____

_____

_____

4. _____

5. _____

6. _____

7. _____

8. _____

Match the transformation of $f(x) = x$ with its graph. Then write a rule for g.

8. $g(x) = -4f(x) + 5$ 9. $g(x) = 4f(x) - 5$ 10. $g(x) = -5f(x) + 4$

A.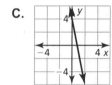

B.

C.

9. _____

_____

10. _____

_____

11. _____

11. A local grocery store makes a 9-pound mixture of trail mix. The trail mix contains raisins, sunflower seeds, and chocolate-covered peanuts. The raisins cost $2 per pound, the sunflower seeds cost $1 per pound, and the chocolate-covered peanuts cost $1.50 per pound. The mixture calls for twice as many raisins as sunflower seeds. The total cost of the mixture is $14.50. How much of each ingredient did the store use?

_____

_____

Chapter 1 **Test A** (continued)

Graph the function and its parent function. Then describe the transformation. *Answers*

12. $f(x) = x - 5$ **13.** $g(x) = 2 + |x|$ **14.** $h(x) = -\frac{1}{3}x^2$

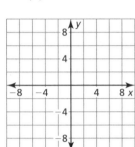 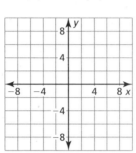 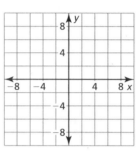

12. ___See left.___

_____

_____

_____

13. ___See left.___

_____

_____

_____

14. ___See left.___

_____

15. The table below shows the amount of fuel left in your RV while driving. What type of function can you use to model the data? Estimate the amount of fuel left in your tank after driving for 90 minutes.

Time (minutes), x	0	20	40	60	80
Fuel left (gallons), y	18	16	14	12	10

_____

_____

_____

Write a function g whose graph represents the indicated transformation of the graph f.

16. $f(x) = -3|x + 1| - 4$; translation 3 units up

17. $f(x) = \frac{2}{3}x^2 + 2$; vertical stretch by a factor of 3

18. Let the graph of g be a horizontal shrink by a factor of $\frac{1}{2}$, followed by a translation 3 units down of the graph of $f(x) = |x|$. Write a rule for g.

19. For your career project, you plan to design and sell T-shirts. During the first 5 weeks of selling the shirts, the function $f(s) = \frac{4}{3}s - 20$ models your profit made, where s is the number of shirts sold. Your teacher mentions that by making a slight change to your printing procedure, you could double the number of shirts you could sell. Find your new profit equation and describe how this change transforms the graph of f. Then determine the new profit you could make by selling 300 shirts.

15. _____

_____

16. _____

17. _____

18. _____

19. _____

_____

_____

Name_____ Date_____

Chapter 1 Test B

Write an equation of the line and interpret the slope and *y*-intercept.

1.

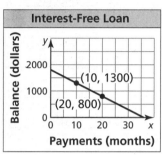

2.

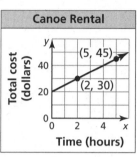

3.

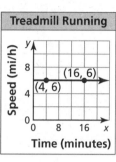

Answers

1. _____

_____

_____

2. _____

_____

_____

_____

3. _____

_____

_____

Solve the system. Check your solution, if possible.

4. $x + y + 3z = -4$
$-x - y - 2z = 5$
$2x - z = -3$

5. $x - 3y - z = -9$
$-2x + y + 2z = 3$
$2x + y + 3z = 8$

6. $x + y + z = 7$
$x - y + 2z = 7$
$2x + 3z = 14$

7. $-x - y - 2z = 9$
$-2x - 2y - z = 1$
$-x - y + z = -10$

4. _____

5. _____

6. _____

Match the transformation of $f(x) = x$ with its graph. Then write a rule for g.

8. $g(x) = -f(x) + 3$ **9.** $g(x) = 3f(x) - 1$ **10.** $g(x) = -3f(x) + 1$

7. _____

8. _____

A.

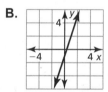

B.

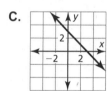

C.

9. _____

10. _____

11. A Major League Baseball stadium sells three types of tickets. Reserved tickets are sold for $20 each, field-level tickets are sold for $50 each, and box seat tickets are sold for $100 each. You purchase 10 total tickets for $370. You have twice as many reserved tickets as field-level tickets. How many tickets of each do you have?

_____

11. _____

_____

_____

_____

Name _____ Date _____

Graph the function and its parent function. Then describe the transformation.   *Answers*

12. $f(x) = 2x^2$ **13.** $f(x) = -x + 6$ **14.** $f(x) = -3|x|$

12. _____See left._____

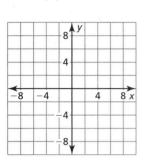 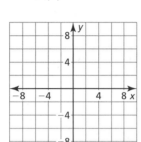 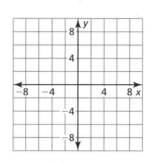

_____

_____

_____

13. _____See left._____

15. The table below shows the height of a football over time after it has been kicked in the air. What type of function can you use to model the data? Estimate the height of the football after 8 seconds.

_____

_____

14. _____See left._____

Time (seconds), x	0	1	2	3	4	5
Height (feet), y	3	52	87	108	115	108

_____

_____

Write a function g whose graph represents the indicated transformation of the graph f.

_____

15. _____

16. $f(x) = -2|x - 1|$; reflection in the y-axis

_____

17. $f(x) = 2x + 5$; translation 2 units up

16. _____

18. Let the graph of g be a vertical stretch by a factor of 3, followed by a translation 2 units up of the graph of $f(x) = x^2$. Write a rule for g.

17. _____

18. _____

19. Your friend is watching as you hit a golf ball. The flight of the ball can be modeled by the equation $f(t) = -7t^2 + 70t + 3$, where t represents time (in seconds) as the ball travels through the air. After hitting your shot, your friend claims that if you strike the ball $\frac{1}{2}$ as hard, your shot will be more precise. Find your new shot equation and describe how this change transforms the graph of f. How high will the ball be 6 seconds after contact using your new swing?

19. _____

_____

_____

Chapter 1 Alternative Assessment

1. The graph shows a system of equations.

   a. What parent functions do you see in the system? What transformations were applied to $f(x)$? to $g(x)$?

   b. Write the equation for $f(x)$.

   c. Write the equation for $g(x)$.

   d. Write the system of equations.

   e. What are the solutions to this system of equations?

   f. Verify your solutions are correct.

2. The table shows the average life expectancy y (in years) of a person born in the United States based on his or her year of birth, x.

Year of birth, x	1920	1930	1940	1950	1960	1970	1980	1990	2000	2010
Life expectancy (years), y	54.1	59.7	62.9	68.2	69.7	70.8	73.7	75.4	77	78.6

   a. Draw a scatter plot of the data using the year of birth as the independent variable and life expectancy as the dependent variable. What type of relationship do the data show?

   b. Use your calculator to find the line of best fit for the data.

   c. What is the correlation coefficient? What does this tell you about the linear model?

   d. Using your model, predict the life expectancy of a person born in the United States in the year 2020. Does your answer seem realistic?

   e. Predict the life expectancy of a person born in 3000. Does your answer seem realistic? Why or why not? Explain why the model could be misleading for this data point. What trends in the data support this?

Name _____ Date _____

Alternative Assessment Rubric

Score	Conceptual Understanding	Mathematical Skills	Work Habits
4	Shows complete understanding of • Applying transformations to parent functions • Solving a system of equations graphically • Creating and using a linear regression model	Writes correct equations, explains transformations, specifies and verifies both correct solutions to system in all of Exercise 1 Graphs scatter plot and writes linear model correctly Includes correct calculations, and discusses data points and trends thoroughly	Answers all parts of both problems All equations and graphs are written or drawn carefully and systematically. Work is very neat and well organized.
3	Shows nearly complete understanding of • Applying transformations to parent functions • Solving a system of equations graphically • Creating and using a linear regression model	Writes correct equations, explains transformations, specifies and verifies both correct solutions to system in most of Exercise 1 Graphs scatter plot or writes linear model correctly Includes at least one correct calculation, and discusses data points and trends	Answers several parts of both problems Most equations and graphs are written or drawn carefully and systematically. Work is neat and organized.
2	Shows some understanding of • Applying transformations to parent functions • Solving a system of equations graphically • Creating and using a linear regression model	Writes correct equations, explains transformations, specifies and verifies both correct solutions to system in some of Exercise 1 Attempts to graph scatter plot and linear model Does not include correct calculations; Discusses briefly either data points or trends	Answers some parts of both problems Equations and graphs are written or drawn carelessly. Work is not very neat or organized.
1	Shows little understanding of • Applying transformations to parent functions • Solving a system of equations graphically • Creating and using a linear regression model	Does not answer Exercise 1 Does not graph scatter plot or write linear model Does not include calculations or discuss data	Does not attempt any part of either problem No equations or graphs are written or drawn. Work is sloppy and disorganized.

Name_____ Date _____

Performance Task

Secret of the Hanging Baskets

Instructional Overview	
Launch Question	A carnival game uses two baskets hanging from springs at different heights. Next to the higher basket is a pile of baseballs. Next to the lower basket is a pile of golf balls. The object of the game is to add the same number of balls to each basket so that the baskets have the same height. But there is a catch—you only get one chance. What is the secret to winning the game?
Summary	The height of each basket can be represented as a linear function dependent on the number of balls in the basket. The two functions become a system of equations. The solution to the system represents an equal number of balls for each basket (the independent variable) which lowers both baskets to an equal height (the dependent variable).
Teacher Notes	Students may not initially recognize that the behavior of the baskets is a system of linear equations. Guide them to this concept by first discussing each basket individually and then as a system.
	Students will quickly believe that the baskets can be set to equal heights with a different number of balls in each basket. The key to understanding this task is that the baskets can be lowered to equal heights with the same number of balls in each basket.
Supplies	Calculators, straightedges or rulers
Mathematical Discourse	What are some common carnival games? Of those, which games are you most likely to win? What is your strategy when you play those games?
Journal/Discussion Prompts	1. Are you certain that this game will have a winner? Why or why not?
	2. Why is the basket associated with the lighter ball lower to start with? (Or, equivalently, why is the basket associated with the heavier ball higher initially?)
	3. Why are the slopes in each equation negative? What does that represent?

Chapter 1 **Performance Task** (continued)

Secret of the Hanging Baskets

Curriculum Content	
CCSSM Content Standards	HSA-CED.2, HSA-CED.3, HSA-REI.5, HSA-REI.6, HSA-REI.11, HSF-IF.5, HSF-BF.1, HSF-LE.2
CCSSM Mathematical Practices	1. Make sense of problems and persevere in solving them: Students recognize that the change in height of the baskets with respect to the number of balls in them is constant, so it can be represented by a line. Because the slopes are not equal, the system has a solution. 4. Model with mathematics: Students use data points to calculate slopes to arrive at a system of linear equations. Students explain the physical difference between a solution to a system of equations and a single equation.

Rubric

Secret of the Hanging Baskets	Points	
Discusses algebraic and physical representation of solution 3. Because the slopes are not equal, the lines will intersect. Their intersection represents the point at which an equal number of balls lowers the baskets to an equal height.	**3** **2** **1**	The answer is well written and correct. The explanation is brief. Only the answer is stated.
Has correct equation of lines 4. Baseball basket equation: $y = -\frac{7}{5}x + 54$ Golf ball basket equation: $y = -\frac{4}{5}x + 45$	**5** **3** **1**	Both equations are correct. One equation is correct. Neither equation is correct.
Has correct solution to system of equations 5. Solution: (15, 33); When 15 balls are put into each basket, they both lower to 33 inches above the ground.	**2** **1**	The solution is correct. The solution is incorrect.
Solves for x-intercept correctly for both lines 6. A total of 39 baseballs and 57 golf balls lowers each basket to the ground. These points represent the x-intercepts of the graphs.	**3** **2** **1**	Both solutions are correct. One solution is correct. Neither solution is correct.
Explains difference between single equation and system 7. The solution to the system is where the lines intersect each other. The x-coordinate is the number of balls needed to lower both baskets to an equal height, and the y-coordinate is that height. The solutions to the individual equations are the x-intercepts, the points at which $y = 0$ or, physically, the points at which the baskets hit the ground.	**2** **1**	Both concepts are explained. One concept is discussed.
Mathematics Practice: Select one of the listed practices to evaluate. This component could be evaluated by interview or observation.	**2**	For demonstration of practice; Partial credit can be awarded.
Total Points	**17 points**	

Name_____ Date_____

Secret of the Hanging Baskets

A carnival game uses two baskets hanging from springs at different heights. Next to the higher basket is a pile of baseballs. Next to the lower basket is a pile of golf balls. The object of the game is to add the same number of balls to each basket so that the baskets have the same height. But there is a catch—you only get one chance. What is the secret to winning the game?

Part 1: The Model

Initially, the empty baseball basket hangs so that the bottom of the basket is at the 54-inch mark, whereas the bottom of the empty golf ball basket hangs at the 45-inch mark.

1. On a separate sheet of paper, sketch the baskets as they look at the beginning of a turn. One contestant puts 10 balls in each basket. This lowers the baseball basket to 40 inches and the golf ball basket to 37 inches. Because the baskets are not at equal height, the contestant does not win. On the same sketch, draw the baskets after this contestant's turn. The baskets are emptied and another contestant puts five balls in each basket. This lowers the baseball basket to 47 inches and the golf ball basket to 41 inches. This contestant does not win either.

2. Plot the data points for each basket in the coordinate plane. Use a straightedge to draw one line through the points plotted for the baseball basket, and one line through the points plotted for the golf ball basket. What is the independent variable? What is the dependent variable? How did you decide on the scale of each axis? Describe what you see in your graphs.

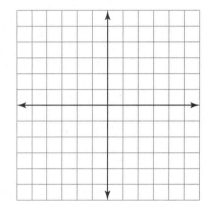

3. Do these lines ever cross? Why? What does the intersection of these two lines represent with respect to the carnival game?

4. Write an equation for each basket representing the height of the basket in terms of the number of balls in the basket.

5. Solve this system of equations. How many balls are needed in each basket to win? What height will the baskets lower on the winning play?

Part 2: Using Your Results

6. How many baseballs do you need to place in the higher basket so that it touches the ground? How many golf balls do you need to place in the lower basket so that it touches the ground? What do these points represent on the graph?

7. Explain the mathematical differences between the solution to the system of equations in Question 5 and the solutions to the single equations in Question 6.

Name _____ Date _____

Describe the transformation of $f(x) = x^2$ represented by g.

Answers

1.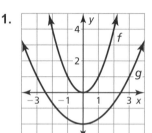
2.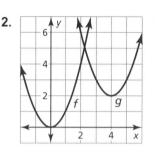
3.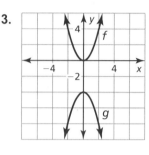

1. _____

_____

2. _____

_____

3. _____

Write a rule for g and identify the vertex.

4. Let g be a translation 2 units up, followed by a reflection in the x-axis and a vertical stretch by a factor of 4 of the graph of $f(x) = x^2$.

5. Let g be a horizontal shrink by a factor of $\frac{1}{3}$, followed by a translation 2 units up and 4 units left of the graph of $f(x) = (3x - 2)^2 + 5$.

Graph the function. Label the vertex and axis of symmetry.

6. $f(x) = 3(x - 4)^2 + 2$ 7. $f(x) = 5x^2 + 4x - 1$

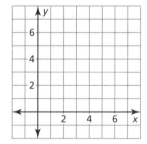   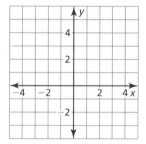

4. _____

_____

5. _____

_____

6. _____See left._____

7. _____See left._____

8. _____

_____

_____

9. _____

_____

_____

10. _____

11. _____

Find the x-intercepts of the graph of the function. Then describe where the function is increasing and decreasing.

8. $g(x) = -1(x - 4)(x + 2)$ 9. $g(x) = \frac{1}{4}(x - 6)(x - 3)$

10. An object is launched directly overhead at 36 meters per second. The height (in meters) of the object is given by $h(t) = -16t^2 + 36t + 5$, where t is the time (in seconds) since the object was launched. For how many seconds is the object at or above a height of 25 meters?

11. A model rocket is launched from the top of a building. The height (in meters) of the rocket above the ground is given by $h(t) = -6t^2 + 24t + 14$, where t is the time (in seconds) since the rocket was launched. What is the rocket's maximum height?

Name_____ Date _____

Answers

1. A parabola has an axis of symmetry $x = -2$ and passes through the point $(-5, 6)$. Find another point that lies on the graph of the parabola.

1. _____

2. Let the graph of g be a vertical stretch by a factor of 4 and a reflection in the x-axis of the graph of $f(x) = x^2 - 3$. Write a rule for g.

2. _____

3. _____

3. Let the graph of g be a translation 1 unit down and 3 units left of the graph of $f(x) = |x - 4| + 2$. Write a rule for g.

4. _____

4. Identify the focus, directrix, and axis of symmetry of $f(x) = \frac{1}{16}x^2$.

_____

_____

5. Explain why a quadratic function models the data. Then use a linear system to find the model.

5. _____

x	1	2	3	4	5
f(x)	−2	2	10	22	38

_____

_____

Write the equation of the parabola.

6.

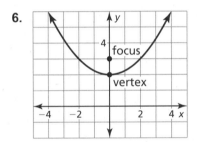

7.

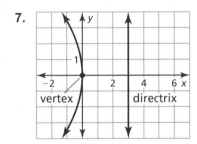

6. _____

7. _____

8. _____

9. _____

10. _____

8.

9.

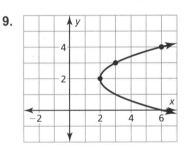

_____

_____

10. Identify the focus, directrix, and axis of symmetry of $x = -\frac{1}{2}y^2$. Then graph the equation.

Chapter 2 **Test A** (continued)

11. A bridge builder plans to construct a cable suspension bridge in your town. The cable being used will form a curve modeled by the equation $h(x) = 3x^2 - 6x + 200$, where x represents the length of cable used (in feet) and $h(x)$ represents the height of the cable (in feet). At what height will the cable hang closest to the bridge deck?

Answers

11. _____

12. ___See left.___

_____

_____

13. ___See left.___

_____

_____

14. _____

15. _____

12. Graph $f(x) = 3(x + 1)^2 - 3$.
    Label the vertex and axis of symmetry. Describe where the function is increasing and decreasing.

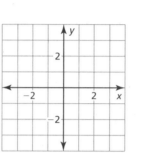

13. Graph $g(x) = -2x^2 - 4x + 3$.
    Label the vertex and axis of symmetry. Describe where the function is increasing and decreasing.

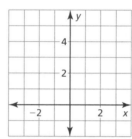

14. At a recent sporting event, you noticed the microphones being used to record the sounds of the event. A drawing of a microphone used is shown to the right. The microphone is placed 8 inches away from the reflector at the focus of the parabola to collect sound. Write an equation that represents the cross section of the parabolic reflector, assuming the vertex is at the origin and the parabola opens right, as shown.

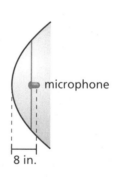

microphone

8 in.

15. The tables show the number of toy bears a toy manufacturer can sell.

Price (dollars), *x*	3	4	5	6	7
Bears sold (in thousands), *y*	84	96	100	96	84

Use quadratic regression to determine how many bears the manufacturer will sell if it charges $9 for each bear.

Name_____ Date_____

Chapter 2 Test B

1. A parabola has an axis of symmetry $y = -4$ and passes through the point $(2, -1)$. Find another point that lies on the graph of the parabola.

2. Let the graph of g be a horizontal shrink by a factor of $\frac{1}{3}$, followed by a translation 1 unit up of the graph of $f(x) = x^2$. Write a rule for g.

3. Let the graph of g be a translation 2 units up and 2 units right, followed by a reflection in the y-axis of the graph of $f(x) = -(x + 3)^2 - 2$. Write a rule for g.

4. Identify the focus, directrix, and axis of symmetry of $x = -\frac{1}{20}y^2$.

5. Explain why a quadratic function models the data. Then use a linear system to find the model.

x	2	4	6	8	10
f(x)	3	33	87	165	267

Write the equation of the parabola.

6.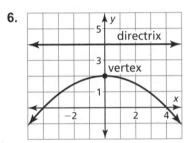

7.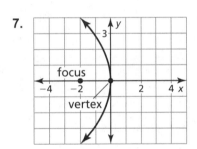

8.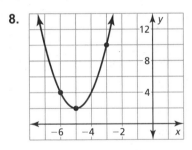

9.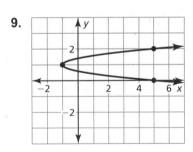

10. Identify the focus, directrix, and axis of symmetry of $f(x) = -\frac{1}{12}x^2$. Then graph the equation.

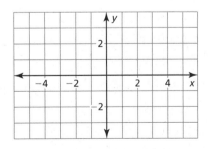

Answers

1. _____

2. _____

3. _____

4. _____

_____

_____

_____

5. _____

_____

_____

6. _____

7. _____

8. _____

9. _____

10. _____

_____

_____

See left. _____

Chapter 2 **Test B** (continued)

11. Your class council determined that its profit from the upcoming homecoming dance is directly related to the ticket price for the dance. Looking at past dances, the council determined that the profit p can be modeled by the function $p(t) = -12t^2 + 480t + 30$, where t represents the price of each ticket. What should be the price of a ticket to the homecoming dance to maximize the council's profit?

12. Graph $f(x) = -(x - 2)^2 + 4$.

    Label the vertex and axis of symmetry. Describe where the function is increasing and decreasing.

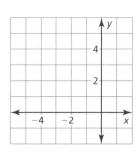

13. Graph $g(x) = \frac{1}{2}x^2 + 2x + 4$.

    Label the vertex and axis of symmetry. Describe where the function is increasing and decreasing.

Answers

11. _____

12. __See left.__

    _____

    _____

13. __See left.__

    _____

    _____

14. _____

15. _____

14. A factory is producing a mirror in the shape of a parabola to be used in searchlights. A drawing of the mirror is shown. The light from the searchlight is located at the focus of the parabola, and will shine through at the given vertex of the mirror. Find an equation that represents the parabolic mirror.

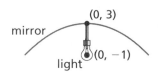

15. A biologist took a count of spotted trout that migrate to the south end of a lake during the winter months. The table shows the population count at the south end of the lake after week 10.

Week, x	2	4	6	8	10
Population, y	185	209	229	209	185

Use quadratic regression to estimate the number of spotted trout at the south end of the lake after week 14.

Chapter 2 Alternative Assessment

1. Which of the following quadratic functions have minimum values? Which have maximum values? Which have the same vertex? Which have the same range?

   a. $f(x) = 2(x + 2)^2 - 2$

   b. $y = -2x^2 - 4x - 4$

   c. $f(x) = (x + 3)(x - 1)$

   d. $y = -(x + 1)^2 - 2$

   e. $f(x) = x^2 + 4x$

   f. $y = 2(x + 1)^2 - 2$

2. A communications company has built a parabolic receiver for an experiment onboard a space shuttle. The receiver has a cross section that satisfies the equation $y = \frac{1}{8}x^2$. The electronics are positioned at the focus of the receiver for the best reception. However, when the final design for the cargo bay is completed, NASA informs the engineers that they now have less depth for the receiver, so they must flatten their design.

   a. What transformation must the engineers apply to their receiver?

   b. What effect does this have on the distance between the vertex of the receiver and the electronics? Why?

   c. What is a possible equation for the new receiver?

3. During training, a hurdler wants to raise the height of the hurdles from the high school standard of 39 inches to the NCAA standard of 42 inches. His best race from last season included a clear over a 39-inch hurdle that was modeled by $h(t) = (-0.025t)(t - 25)$, where t is time (in tenths of a second) after his lead leg left the track.

   a. If he runs as well as his best race last year, will this hurdler clear the new height? Why or why not?

   b. Why must the quadratic term in this model have a negative coefficient?

Name _____ Date _____

Score	Conceptual Understanding	Mathematical Skills	Work Habits
4	Shows complete understanding of: • the vertex of a parabola, calculating it, and classifying it as a maximum or minimum • identifying the focus and directrix of a parabola	Correctly answers all questions in Exercise 1 Identifies correct transformation and explains its effect on the parabola Correctly answers and explains solution to Exercise 3	Answers all parts of all problems Answers are explained thoroughly with mathematical terminology Work is very neat and well organized
3	Shows nearly complete understanding of: • the vertex of a parabola, calculating it and classifying it as a maximum or minimum • identifying the focus and directrix of a parabola	Correctly answers most questions in Exercise 1 Identifies correct transformation but does not explain its effect Correctly answers but does not explain solution to Exercise 3	Answers most parts of all problems Answers are explained with mathematical terminology Work is neat and organized
2	Shows some understanding of: • the vertex of a parabola, calculating it and classifying it as a maximum or minimum • identifying the focus and directrix of a parabola	Correctly answers some questions in Exercise 1 Incorrectly identifies transformation Incorrectly answers Exercise 3	Answers some parts of all problems Answers are poorly or incorrectly explained Work is not very neat or organized
1	Shows little understanding of: • the vertex of a parabola, calculating it and classifying it as a maximum or minimum • identifying the focus and directrix of a parabola	Does not answer Exercise 1 Does not specify transformation for Exercise 2 Does not clearly answer Exercise 3	Attempts few parts of any problem No explanation is included with answers Work is sloppy and disorganized

Name_____ Date _____

 Chapter 2 **Performance Task**

Accident Reconstruction

Instructional Overview	
Launch Question	Was the driver of a car speeding when the brakes were applied? What do skid marks at the scene of an accident reveal about the moments before the collision?
Summary	The relationship between velocity (speed) and braking distance is quadratic. Using real data and quadratic regression, students will model the relationship between velocity and braking distance, and calculate the braking distance for common speed limits. Then students will use dimensions of a known object in a photograph, such as the length of the dashed lines along a road, to estimate a scale. Using this scale, they will measure the length of skid marks to determine the braking distance, and they will compare this with their table to determine the minimum speed.
Teacher Notes	Part 1 can be done individually or in groups. Encourage students to consider what it means for braking distance to increase quadratically with speed. Is this shown in the scatter plot? Ask them how braking distance would increase with speed if this relationship were linear.
	The resulting regression is: $D_B = 0.04445x^2 - 0.0005x + 0.01$, with $R^2 = 1$. Have the students run a linear regression on this data also. This regression yields $R^2 = 0.97$. Discuss what this means about the model.
	Part 2 is best completed in groups. To measure the skid marks, students can compare them to the dashed road lines in the scene. The standard length of dashed road lines and spaces are given in the task. The dashes seem to decrease in length at the top of the picture due to the perspective of distance. Encourage students to discuss how they will handle this in their measurements. Provide string, index cards, rulers, and other material for measuring.
Supplies	Calculators, string, index cards, rulers, and other measuring materials, additional photographs if desired
Discussion/Writing Prompts	1. Given a photograph, how can we determine the actual size of objects in the picture?
	2. In our model for braking distance, why is the velocity a *minimum* speed?
	3. What assumptions are we making about our data and the conditions in which it was collected?
	4. What is the difference between braking distance and stopping distance?
	5. What does it mean for a relationship between a dependent and independent variable to be quadratic?
	6. Interpret your mathematical model in words. What does it mean for your own driving?

Name _____ Date _____

 Performance Task (continued)

Accident Reconstruction

Curriculum Content	
CCSSM Content Standards	HSA-CED.2, HSA-CED.4, HSF-IF.4, HSF-IF.5
CCSSM Mathematical Practices	1. Make sense of problems and persevere in solving them: Students recognize that before they can interpret the skid marks, they must first define a scale as a reference for their measurement. 4. Model with mathematics: Students use real data and quadratic regression to construct an equation for braking distance in terms of velocity. 5. Use appropriate tools strategically: Students will use calculators to perform quadratic regression and rulers to interpret key information in a picture.

Name_____ Date_____

Rubric

Accident Reconstruction	Points	
Part 1: Has correct scatter plot (Axes' scales will vary.)	3	Correct with axes labeled
	2	Correct with no labels
	1	Some points graphed correctly
Has correct equation for braking distance: $D_B = 0.04445x^2 - 0.005x + 0.01$ with $R^2 = 1$	3	All 3 coefficients correct
	2	2 coefficients correct
	1	1 coefficient correct
Discusses fit of model	3	R^2 is compared between linear and quadratic models.
	2	R^2 is mentioned, but not compared.
	1	R^2 is not included.
Correctly completes table Answers will vary with round-off error of model. Approximate answer: $25 \rightarrow 27.78$, $35 \rightarrow 54.44$, $55 \rightarrow 134.44$, $65 \rightarrow 187.78$, $75 \rightarrow 250.00$	3	All correct
	2	Up to 2 incorrect
	1	Up to 4 incorrect
Part 2: Explanation of measurement method	5	Well-written and thorough
	3	Writing is brief or incomplete
	1	A method is listed but not explained.
Final answer will vary based on skid measurement and chosen road type	5	Well-written and thorough
	3	Writing is brief or incomplete
	1	An answer is listed but not explained.
Mathematics Practice: Select one of the listed practices to evaluate. This component could be evaluated from observation of the student or team working.	3	Demonstration of the practice; Partial credit can be awarded.
Total Points	**25 points**	

Chapter 2 **Performance Task** (continued)

Accident Reconstruction

Was the driver of a car speeding when the brakes were applied? What do skid marks at the scene of an accident reveal about the moments before the collision?

Part 1: The Model

Few drivers know their true speed in the moments before an accident, but tire skid marks at the scene are a good clue. Skid marks occur when hard braking is applied, which causes tires to stop turning. The distance a car travels after brakes are applied until it comes to rest is called braking distance. Braking distance increases quadratically with respect to the speed of the vehicle.

1. Make a scatter plot of braking data. Be sure to label your axes. For our model, we will consider the basic conditions for braking distance and will assume an average-sized car is traveling on a dry, paved surface.

Velocity (miles per hour)	Braking distance (feet)
20	17.78
30	40
40	71.11
50	111.11
60	160
70	217.78

Chapter 2 **Performance Task** (continued)

2. Use quadratic regression to define an equation for braking distance in terms of velocity.

   D_B = _____

   How closely does your model match the data according to the R^2 value?

   Compare this to a linear regression run on the same data. Which is the better fit?

   Using your model, complete the table for common road speeds. Note that legal speed limits vary by state and municipality.

Road type	Velocity (miles per hour)	Braking distance (feet)
residential	25	
business district	35	
undivided highway	55	
divided highway	65	
freeway/interstate	75	

Name _____ Date _____

Part 2: Using Your Results

How could you estimate the minimum speed of the car that made the skid marks in this picture? What additional information do you need to know?

A helpful fact is that each dashed line on any road or highway is 10 feet long, with 30 feet in between dashes.

Why do the dashed road lines appear smaller near the top of the picture? How will you adjust for this in making your measurement?

Once you have determined a scale (or scales) for the picture, measure the skid marks.

Given the length of the skid marks, what was the approximate minimum speed of the vehicle when the brakes were applied? Was the driver speeding? Explain your answer.

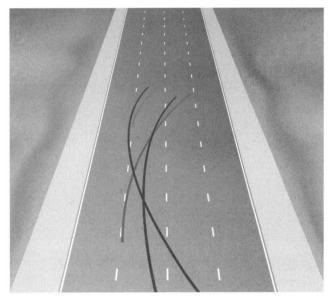

Chapter 2 **Performance Task** (continued)

Teacher Notes:

Name _____ Date _____

Solve the equation by using the graph. Check your solution(s).

Answers

1. $x^2 - x - 12 = 0$ 2. $2x^2 - 4 = -7x$ 3. $x^2 = 5x - 6$

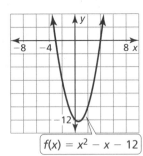 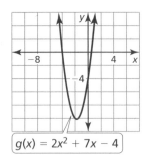 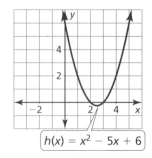

$f(x) = x^2 - x - 12$ $g(x) = 2x^2 + 7x - 4$ $h(x) = x^2 - 5x + 6$

Solve the equation using square roots or by factoring.

4. $x^2 = 3x - 1$ 5. $x(x - 1) = 3$ 6. $2(x^2 - 2x) = 5$

7. Find the values of x and y that satisfy the equation $5x + 8i = 30 + yi$.

Perform the operation. Write your answer in standard form.

8. $(3 + 4i) + (-6 + 2i)$ 9. $(7 + 6i) - (4 - 3i)$

10. Find the zeros of the function $f(x) = 5x^2 + 2$.

Solve the equation by completing the square.

11. $x^2 + 16x - 22 = 0$ 12. $x^2 - 12x + 26 = 0$

13. Write $y = x^2 + 4x - 5$ in vertex form. Then identify the vertex.

14. A water balloon is tossed into the air so that its height h (in feet) after t seconds can be modeled by the function $h(t) = -16t^2 + 80t + 5$.

    a. What is the height of the balloon after 1 second?

    b. For how long is the balloon more than 30 feet high?

    c. What is the maximum height of the balloon?

15. A rectangular lawn measuring 24 feet by 16 feet is surrounded by a flower bed of uniform width. The combined area of the lawn and the flower bed is 660 square feet. What is the width of the flower bed?

1. _____

2. _____

3. _____

4. _____

5. _____

6. _____

7. _____

8. _____

9. _____

10. _____

11. _____

12. _____

13. _____

_____

14. a. _____

b. _____

c. _____

15. _____

Name_____ Date_____

Chapter 3 **Test A**

Solve the equation using any method.

Answers

1. $x^2 + 16x + 60 = 0$

2. $x^2 + 4x + 4 = 49$

3. $-4x^2 + 6x - 2 = 0$

4. $3x^2 + 22x = -35$

5. $49x^2 + 4 = 0$

6. $6x^2 - 54 = 0$

Use the graph to determine the number and type of solutions of the quadratic equation.

7.
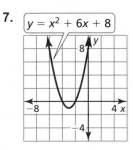
$y = x^2 + 6x + 8$

8.
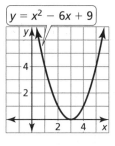
$y = x^2 - 6x + 9$

9.
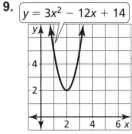
$y = 3x^2 - 12x + 14$

10.
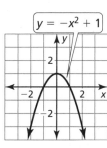
$y = -x^2 + 1$

1. _____

2. _____

3. _____

4. _____

5. _____

6. _____

7. _____

8. _____

9. _____

10. _____

11. a._____

  b._____

12. _____

13. _____

11. The Freedom Tower in New York City is 1776 feet tall. The equation $f(t) = -16t^2 + 1776$ models the height $f(t)$ (in feet) of an object t seconds after it is dropped from the top of the tower.

   a. After how many seconds will the object hit the ground? Round your answer to the nearest hundredth of a second.

   b. What is the height of the object 3 seconds after it has been dropped from the top of the tower?

12. Write $(-2 - 5i) - (-4 + 2i)$ as a complex number in standard form.

13. Write $(3 - 3i)(1 - 6i)$ as a complex number in standard form.

Name _____ Date _____

Solve the system of equations.

Answers

14. $y = -2x^2 - 6$

$y = -(x - 3)^2 + 8$

15. $8x + y = -2x^2 - 8$

$x^2 - y - 6x = -10$

Graph the inequality.

16. $y \geq -x^2 - 4$

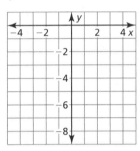

Graph the system of quadratic inequalities.

17. $y + x^2 \leq 2$

$y - x^2 - 2x + 6 > 0$

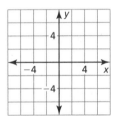

14. _____

15. _____

16. ___See left.___

17. ___See left.___

18. _____

19. _____

20. _____

18. A toy rocket is fired straight into the air. The rocket has an initial velocity of 48 feet per second and its height is modeled by the equation $h(t) = 480t - 16t^2$, where h is the height (in feet) and t is the time (in seconds). At what time will the toy rocket reach its maximum height?

19. A carpenter is cutting a board to make a brace on a wall that will be used in a house. The shape of the brace will be a right triangle. In order for the brace to fit, the legs of the brace must be in a ratio of 3:2. The hypotenuse must be 26 inches long. What will the lengths of the legs be? Round your answers to the nearest tenth of an inch.

20. You and a friend decide to go into business selling bobblehead dolls. The profit p for selling b bobblehead dolls is given by the equation $p(b) = -0.2b^2 + 15b - 150$. How many bobblehead dolls will you have to sell for your profit to be greater than $100?

Name_____ Date _____

Solve the equation using any method.

Answers

1. $x^2 + 12x + 35 = 0$
2. $3x^2 - 48 = 0$

3. $x^2 + 10x + 25 = 64$
4. $-3x^2 - 5x = 5$

5. $4x^2 + 3x - 10 = 0$
6. $36x^2 + 49 = 0$

Use the graph to determine the number and type of solutions of the quadratic equation.

7.
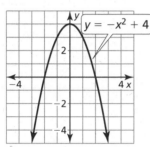
$y = -x^2 + 4$

8.
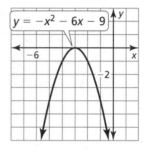
$y = -x^2 - 6x - 9$

9.
$y = 3x^2 - 12x + 14$

10.
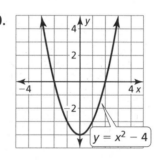
$y = x^2 - 4$

1. _____
2. _____
3. _____
4. _____
5. _____
6. _____
7. _____
8. _____
9. _____
10. _____
11. _____
12. _____
13. _____

11. A golf ball is hit from the ground, and its height can be modeled by the equation $h(t) = -16t^2 + 128t$, where $h(t)$ represents the height (in feet) of the ball t seconds after contact. What will the maximum height of the ball be?

12. Write $(1 - i) - (4 - 5i)$ as a complex number in standard form.

13. Write $(-4 + 5i)(5 - i)$ as a complex number in standard form.

Chapter 3 Test B (continued)

Solve the system of equations.

14. $-2x^2 + y = 1$

$\quad\quad y = (x - 1)^2 + 3$

15. $4x - y = 4$

$\quad\quad x^2 - y = -1$

Graph the inequality.

16. $3x^2 - y > 5$

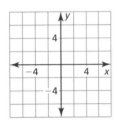

Graph the system of quadratic inequalities.

17. $x + y^2 > 3$

$\quad\quad -3x + y < 1$

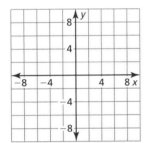

18. A company that produces video games has hired you to set the sale price for its newest game. Based on production costs and consumer demand, the company has concluded that the equation $p(x) = -0.3x^2 + 45x - 1000$ represents the profit p (in dollars) for x individual games sold. What will the company's profit be if it sells 100 games?

19. A landscaper is designing a flower garden in the shape of a trapezoid. She wants the shorter base to be 3 yards greater than the height and the longer base to be 7 yards greater than the height. The total area of the flower garden is 150 square yards. What will the length of each base be?

20. To begin a basketball game, a referee must toss the ball vertically into the air. This process can be modeled by the equation $h(t) = -16t^2 + 22t + 6$, where h represents the ball's height (in feet) after t seconds. Determine the time interval (in seconds) in which the height of the basketball is greater than 8 feet. Round your answer to the nearest thousandth of a second.

Answers

14. _____

15. _____

16. ___See left.___

17. ___See left.___

18. _____

19. _____

20. _____

Chapter 3 Alternative Assessment

1. Explain how different quadratic functions can have the same zeros. Which of the following have the same zeros?

   a. $f(x) = x^2 + 2x - 3$

   b. $y = (x - 3)(x + 1)$

   c. $f(x) = 2(x + 3)(x - 1)$

   d. $y = -(x + 1)^2 - 2$

   e. $f(x) = -3x^2 - 6x + 9$

   f. $y = (x + 1)^2 - 4$

2. The table shows the annual average yogurt consumption per capita in the United States.

Year, x	1960	1970	1980	1990	2000	2010
Yogurt consumption, y (pints)	0.35	1.6	3.25	4.25	4.95	11.5

   a. Draw a scatter plot of the data using the year as your independent variable. How can you define your axis scale so that your data begins at the origin? Explain how the data appear to fit a quadratic model.

   b. Use the quadratic regression feature of your calculator to find the curve of best fit for the data.

   c. What is the coefficient of determination? What data point(s) keep this coefficient from being higher and why?

   d. Using your model from part (b), does this model have an x-intercept? What does this mean about yogurt consumption in the United States?

   e. Using your model from part (b), predict the average amount of yogurt an American will consume in the year 2020.

   f. Compare the data trends between the 1990s and the 2000s. What factors might influence yogurt consumption in the United States? How would they affect it?

Name _____ Date _____

Chapter 3 | **Alternative Assessment Rubric**

Score	Conceptual Understanding	Mathematical Skills	Work Habits
4	Shows complete understanding of: • Finding roots/zeros of a quadratic function • Creating and using a quadratic regression model	Gives correct and thorough explanation to Exercise 1 Identifies all quadratics with same zeros correctly Calculates correct quadratic model and answer to Exercise 2	Answers all parts of all problems The answers are explained thoroughly with mathematical terminology. Work is very neat and well organized.
3	Shows nearly complete understanding of: • Finding roots/zeros of a quadratic function • Creating and using a quadratic regression model	Gives brief explanation to Exercise 1 Identifies all but one quadratic with same zeros correctly Calculates correct quadratic model but gives incorrect prediction in Exercise 2	Answers most parts of all problems The answers are explained with mathematical terminology. Work is neat and organized.
2	Shows some understanding of: • Finding roots/zeros of a quadratic function • Creating and using a quadratic regression model	Gives incorrect explanation to Exercise 1 Incorrectly chooses several quadratics that do not have same zeros Calculates incorrect quadratic model and gives incorrect prediction in Exercise 2	Answers some parts of all problems The answers are poorly or incorrectly explained. Work is not very neat or organized.
1	Shows little understanding of: • Finding roots/zeros of a quadratic function • Creating and using a quadratic regression model	Omits explanation to Exercise 1 Incorrectly chooses many quadratics that do not have same zeros States incorrect answer with no explanation in Exercise 2	Attempts few parts of any problem No explanation is included with the answers. Work is sloppy and disorganized.

Performance Task

Algebra in Genetics: The Hardy-Weinberg Law

Instructional Overview	
Launch Question	Some people have attached earlobes, the recessive trait. Some people have free earlobes, the dominant trait. What percent of people carry both traits?
Summary	For genes with two alleles, the frequency of genotypes is represented by the quadratic equation $p^2 + 2pq + q^2 = 1$. This is known as the Hardy-Weinberg Law and is derived by squaring each side of the equation $p + q = 1$, where p is the likelihood of carrying one single allele and q is the likelihood of carrying the other. The task begins with an explanation of vocabulary and guides the student through the derivation. Then, using the example of free and attached earlobes, students calculate the likelihood of each genotype.
Teacher Notes	One problem in genetics is that we cannot observe the number of people who carry one recessive gene and one dominant gene. We can only visually identify the number of people who carry two recessive genes, because that is the only genotype that will show the recessive trait. Everyone else has at least one dominant gene, but many have two dominant genes. From this large pool, we must somehow pull out the number of those carrying single recessive genes. The Hardy-Weinberg Law allows us to do this.
	This kind of calculation is critical in monitoring health issues like the number of people who carry a gene for a certain disease or condition.
	Note that the existence of a single gene for free or attached earlobes has not been definitively established, and the example is used solely for illustration in this task.
Supplies	Calculators
Mathematical Discourse	If we look at a group of people with brown eyes, could we determine who also carried a gene for green eyes or blue eyes?
Writing/Discussion Prompts	1. Why is the ability to know how many people carry a certain gene important to world health?
	2. Explain why the only thing we know by observation is whether a person carries two recessive genes for a certain trait.

Chapter 3 **Performance Task** (continued)

Algebra in Genetics: The Hardy-Weinberg Law

Curriculum Content	
CCSSM Content Standards	HSA-CED.1, HSA-CED.2, HSA-SSE.3, HSF-LE.1, HSS-CP.1, HSS-CP.5, HSS-CP.7, HSS-CP.8
CCSSM Mathematical Practices	1. Make sense of problems and persevere in solving them: Students recognize that the only value that can be observed is q^2 even though they need the quantity pq. They must use several mathematical concepts to create the model, and the biological terminology may be new to them. 4. Model with mathematics: Students apply probability and a quadratic equation to determine characteristics of a population.

Rubric

Algebra in Genetics: The Hardy-Weinberg Law	Points	
Part 2: a. $p + q = 1$ b. $(p + q)^2 = 1^2$ c. $p^2 + 2pq + q^2 = 1$	**3** **2** **1**	3 answers correct 2 answers correct 1 answer correct
Part 3: a. p^2 represents the probability of having two dominant **F** alleles, and q^2 represents the probability of having two recessive **a** alleles. b. $2pq$ represents twice the probability of having both alleles, **F** and **a**.	**3** **2** **1**	3 answers correct 2 answers correct 1 answer correct
Part 4: a. **Fa** and **aF** b. **FF, Fa , aF** c. **aa** d. The only observable certainty is that someone with **aa** has attached lobes. Because the probability of one **a** is q, the probability of two **aa** is $q \bullet q = q^2$. This is 20% of the population. e. square root; $q = 0.45$ f. $p = 0.55$ g. $2pq = 0.495$ h. 4950	**7** **5** **2**	All answers correct Most answers correct Few answers correct
Mathematics Practice: Make sense of problems and persevere in solving them. This component could be evaluated by interview or observation.	**2**	For demonstration of practice; Partial credit can be awarded.
Total Points	**15 points**	

Name_____ Date_____

Performance Task (continued)

Algebra in Genetics: The Hardy-Weinberg Law

Some people have attached earlobes, the recessive trait. Some people have free earlobes, the dominant trait. What percent of people carry both traits?

Part 1: Background

Algebra is everywhere—even in your genes! A famous quadratic equation called the Hardy-Weinberg Law can predict the number of people in large populations who carry certain genetic combinations. These combinations are called genotypes.

What is a genotype? Human beings have thousands of genes that determine characteristics such as eye color, hair color, and height. Each gene has different versions called alleles. For example, an ear lobe gene would have an allele for free lobes, earlobes that hang below the point where they attach, and an allele for attached lobes. Humans carry two alleles, one from a mother and one from a father, for each gene. These two alleles together make up a genotype for a specific trait. The possible genotypes for free (F) and attached (a) earlobes are shown in the table.

		Paternal allele	
		F	a
Maternal allele	F	FF	Fa
	a	aF	aa

Because one allele is physically dominant, it is difficult to observe how many people carry *both* alleles. For example, a person with free lobes could have the *FF* genotype, *or* he or she could have the *Fa* or *aF* genotypes. The only thing that is known for sure is that the person with attached lobes carries the *aa* genotype and does *not* have both alleles.

Part 2: Creating the Model

So how can you know how many people carry both alleles? That is where the algebra comes in!

Considering a **single** allele, let

   p = the probability that the single allele is *F*, dominant free lobes, and

   q = the probability that the single allele is *a*, recessive attached lobes.

  a. Because the allele is either one or the other, the chance of having one or the other is 100%. Write a sum that represents this.

   ____ + ____ = 1

  b. However, you need to know something about two alleles. The probability of having both alleles is given by $p \cdot q$. What can you do to the binomial in part (a) to create a term with $p \cdot q$?

   (____ + ____)⁻ = 1⁻

  c. Expand the quadratic equation. This equation is known as the Hardy-Weinberg Law.

   ____ + ____ + ____ = 1

Name _____ Date _____

Part 3: Understanding the Model

Your model now has terms representing *genotypes*, two alleles. Use the fact that you multiply to find the probability of two independent events to answer the following.

   a. What do the quadratic terms represent?

   $p^2 = p \bullet p$ represents

   $q^2 = q \bullet q$ represents

   b. What does the term $2pq$ represent?

Part 4: Using the Model

In a population of 10,000 people, suppose that 80% have free earlobes and 20% have attached earlobes. Remember, you can observe only their *physical* traits. How can you calculate the number of people who carry *both* alleles?

   a. Which genotypes have *both* alleles? Note that you are trying to find the percentage of the population that has these genotypes.

   b. Because free earlobes are dominant, which three genotypes comprise 80% of the population?

   c. Because attached earlobes are recessive, which genotype does 20% of the population have?

   d. Explain how you know that $q^2 = q \bullet q = 0.2$.

   e. Now that you know the numerical value of q^2, what operation will you use to find the numerical value of q? Find q.

   f. Now that you know q, use the equation from part (2a) to find p.

   g. Find $2p \bullet q$, the probability of carrying both alleles. Genotypes with both alleles are *Fa* and *aF*.

   h. In a population of 10,000 people, how many carry *both* alleles?

Performance Task (continued)

Teacher Notes:

Chapters 1–3 Quarterly Standards Based Test

1. Which function does not belong with the other three? *(HSF-BF.3)*

    A. $f(x) = -|x + 2|$

    B. $f(x) = x^2 + 5$

    C. $f(x) = -3(x - 4)^2$

    D. $f(x) = -2|x| - 6$

2. If a function has a domain of all real numbers and a range of $y \geq 3$, which of the following are possible functions? Choose all that apply. *(HSF-BF.3)*

    A. $g(x) = 7x^2 + 3$

    B. $g(x) = -2|x + 4| + 3$

    C. $g(x) = \frac{2}{3}|x - 2| - 3$

    D. $g(x) = 5x + 3$

3. Let $f(x) = 2(x - 5)^2 - 4$. Which of the following functions is a reflection in the y-axis of the graph of f? *(HSF-BF.3)*

    A. $g(x) = -2(x - 5)^2 - 4$

    B. $g(x) = -2(x + 5)^2 - 4$

    C. $g(x) = 2(-x + 5)^2 - 4$

    D. $g(x) = 2(x + 5)^2 - 4$

4. Write a function g whose graph represents the indicated transformation of each graph of f. Use a graphing calculator to check your answers. *(HSF-BF.A.1a)*

    a. $f(x) = 3x^2 - 2$; reflection in the x-axis

    b. $f(x) = (x + 2)^2 - 1$; vertical shrink by a factor of $\frac{1}{5}$

    c. $f(x) = -|x| + 4$; horizontal shrink by a factor of $\frac{1}{4}$

    d. $f(x) = 4x - 7$; translation 3 units left

Chapters 1–3 **Quarterly Standards Based Test** (continued)

5. The function $g(x) = \frac{1}{3}|x + 2| - 5$ is a combination of transformations of $f(x) = |x|$.

Choose which letter describes the transformation. *(HSF-BF.3)*

   A. vertical shift 5 units down, horizontal shift 2 units right, vertical shrink by
      a factor of $\frac{1}{3}$

   B. horizontal shift 2 units left, vertical shrink by a factor of $\frac{1}{3}$, vertical shift
      5 units down

   C. horizontal shift 2 units left, vertical stretch by a factor of 3, vertical shift
      5 units down

   D. horizontal shift 2 units right, vertical stretch by a factor of 3, vertical shift
      5 units down

6. Which equation has a graph that is a line passing through the point $(-3, 7)$ and

   is parallel to the graph of $y = \frac{2}{3}x - 5$? *(HSA-CED.2 and HSF-LE.A.2)*

   A. $y = \frac{2}{3}x + 1$ B. $y = -\frac{3}{2}x + \frac{5}{2}$

   C. $y = \frac{2}{3}x + 9$ D. $y = \frac{3}{2}x + \frac{23}{2}$

7. The data pairs (x, y) represent the number of bait fish y in the tank x minutes after
   the initial throw of the cast net. *(HSS-ID.B.6a, HSA-CED.3, and HSF-LE.B.5)*

   $(0, 75), (1, 99), (2, 122), (3, 142), (4, 171), (5, 193)$

   a. Verify that the data show a linear relationship.

   b. Use the *linear regression* feature on a graphing calculator to find the equation
      of the line of best fit. Estimate the number of bait fish in the tank 24 minutes
      after the initial throw of the cast net.

   c. Interpret the slope and y-intercept in this situation.

   d. Would it make sense to estimate the number of bait fish in the tank 154 minutes
      after the initial throw of the cast net?

Chapters 1–3 **Quarterly Standards Based Test** (continued)

8. Use the *linear regression* feature on a graphing calculator to find an equation of the line of best fit for the data. Find and interpret the correlation coefficient. *(HSS-ID.C.8)*

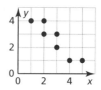

9. Solve the system of linear equations. *(HSA-REI.C.6)*

$$-x - 4y + 2z = -4$$
$$3x + 2y - z = 2$$
$$2x + 3y - 2z = 1$$

10. You and your friend are playing water volleyball. The parabola shows the path of your friend's serve. The path of your serve can be modeled by the function $h(x) = -16x^2 + 32x - 12$. Choose the correct inequality symbol to indicate whose serve travels higher. Explain your reasoning. *(HSF-IF.C.9)*

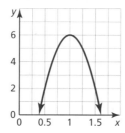

maximum height of your serve ☐ maximum height of your friend's serve

11. Your math team decides to have a dunk tank at the Fall Festival to raise money for team competitions. There is no fee for the water, but the rental fee for the dunk tank is $75. The table shows the profits y (in dollars) when x tickets are sold for the dunk tank. *(HSF-LE.A.2)*

Tickets, x	30	70	110	150	190
Profit, y	−30	30	90	150	210

a. What is the cost per ticket?

b. Your team expects 150 tickets to be sold and finds another dunk tank that rents for only $60. How much should your team charge per ticket to still make the same profit?

c. Your team decides to charge the amount in part (a) and use the less expensive dunk tank. How much more money will your team raise?

Name_____ Date _____

12. Order the following parabolas from greatest width to least width. *(HSF-IF.B.4)*

   a. $y = \frac{1}{6}x^2 - 5$

   b. focus: $(2, 4)$; directrix: $y = 0$

   c. $x = \frac{1}{9}(y + 3)^2$

   d. $y = \frac{2}{5}(x - 10)^2 + 7$

13. Let $g(x) = -f(x)$ and $h(x) = f(-x)$. For which of the following functions is $g(x) = h(x)$? Choose all that apply. *(HSF-BF.B.3)*

   A. $f(x) = x^2$

   B. $f(x) = x$

   C. $f(x) = |x|$

   D. $f(x) = -x$

14. Let the graph of g represent a horizontal shrink and a reflection in the y-axis, followed by a translation right and up of the graph of $f(x) = x^2$. Use the tiles to write a rule for g. *(HSF-BF.B.3)*

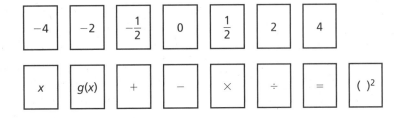

15. Basic Cable Company A charges $30 per month plus a setup fee of $75. Basic Cable Company B charges $40 per month, but due to a special promotion is not currently charging a setup fee. *(HSF-LE.A.2)*

   a. Write an equation for each cable company modeling the total cost y for a subscription lasting x months.

   b. When is it more economical for a person to choose Basic Cable Company B over Basic Cable Company A?

   c. Basic Cable Company A lowers its setup fee to $30. Write the new equation that represents the cost of cable for this company. Describe the transformation this change represents and how it affects your decision in part (b).

Chapters 1–3 **Quarterly Standards Based Test** (continued)

16. Which inequality is shown in the graph? *(HSA-CED.A.3)*

A. $y < -x^2 + 3x + 4$

B. $y \leq -x^2 + 3x + 4$

C. $y < -x^2 - 3x + 4$

D. $y \leq -x^2 - 3x + 4$

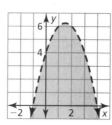

17. Classify each function by its function family. Then describe the transformation of the parent function. *(HSF-BF.B.3)*

a. $g(x) = 7$

b. $h(x) = x^2 + 5$

c. $h(x) = x - 9$

d. $g(x) = \frac{1}{3}|x - 1| + 4$

e. $g(x) = -(x + 6)^2 - 5$

f. $h(x) = 3x - 7$

18. Two osprey dove down to grab two fish near the water surface. The path of each osprey is modeled by the parabolas, where x is the horizontal distance (in feet) from their perch on a tree and y is the height (in feet) above the river floor. The shaded area of the graph represents the possible area of where the fish were located. Choose the correct symbol for each inequality to model the possible locations of the fish near the water surface. *(HSA-CED.A.3)*

First osprey: y ☐ $0.05x^2 - x + 7.5$

Second osprey: y ☐ $0.01x^2 - 0.2x + 6$

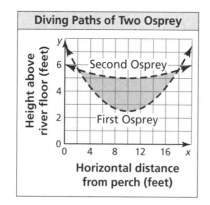

Chapters 1-3 Quarterly Standards Based Test (continued)

19. You claim it is possible to make a function from the given values that has a vertex at $(2, -1)$. Your friend claims it is possible to make a function that has a vertex at $(2, 1)$.

What values can you use to support your claim? What values support your friend's claim? *(HSF-IF.B.4)*

Your Claim
$f(x) = \boxed{}\ x^2 - 8x + \boxed{}$

Your Friend's Claim
$f(x) = \boxed{}\ x^2 - 8x + \boxed{}$

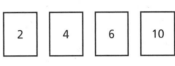

9	7	-5	-1
2	4	6	10

20. Which of the following values are *x*-coordinates of the solutions of the system? *(HSA-REI.C.7)*

$$y = x^2 + 8x - 15$$
$$y = 16x - 27$$

-8	-6	-4	-2
2	4	6	8

21. The table shows the height of the water in a tank where water is being added at a constant rate. How long will it take for the height of the water in the tank to be 250 feet? *(HSF-LE.A.2)*

A. 25 hours

B. 35 hours

C. 45 hours

D. 55 hours

Time (hours), *t*	0	10	20	30	40
Height (feet), *y*	70	110	150	190	230

Name _____ Date _____

Decide whether the function is a polynomial function. If so, write it in standard form and state its degree, type, and leading coefficient.

Answers

1. _____

1. $f(x) = -5x - 10 + 3x^4 + 4x^2$ 2. $h(x) = x^2 - 3x + \dfrac{1}{x} + 4$

_____

_____

3. Describe the x-values for which (a) f is increasing or decreasing, (b) $f(x) > 0$, and (c) $f(x) < 0$.

_____

_____

_____

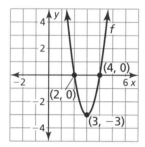

2. _____

_____

_____

_____

4. Write an expression for the area and perimeter for the figure shown.

_____

_____

3. a. _____

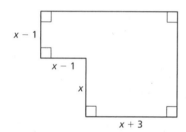

b. _____

c. _____

4. _____

Perform the indicated operation.

5. $(x^2 + 4x - 6)(2x - 4)$ 6. $(5x^2 - 2) - (4x^2 + 6x - 4)$ 5. _____

6. _____

7. Divide $3x^3 - 2x^2 + 4x - 3$ by $x^2 + 3x + 3$.

7. _____

Factor the polynomial completely.

8. _____

8. $4a^2 - 12a + 8$ 9. $5x^4 - 80$ 10. $2z^3 - 3z^2 + 4z - 3$

9. _____

11. Show that $x + 3$ is a factor of $f(x) = 3x^4 - 3x^3 - 36x^2$. Then factor $f(x)$ completely.

10. _____

11. _____

12. The volume V (in cubic inches) of a rectangular cardboard box is modeled by the function $V(x) = (18 - 2x)(3 - 2x)x$, where x is the width (in inches) of the box. Determine the values of x for which the model makes sense. Explain your reasoning.

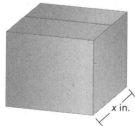

_____

12. _____

_____

Name_____ Date_____

Write a polynomial function *f* of least degree that has rational coefficients, a leading coefficient of 1, and the given zeros.

1. $2, -1, \sqrt{3}$

2. $3, -2, 2i$

Find the product or quotient.

3. $\left(3x^3 + 6x^2 - 5x + 12\right) \div (x - 3)$

4. $\left(3x - 2\right)^3$

5. $(m - 2)(m + 3)(m - 1)$

6. $\left(2x^4 - x^2 + 3x + 1\right) \div \left(x^2 + 2x + 2\right)$

7. $\left(5x + 3\right)^2$

8. $\left(z^5 - 2\right)\left(z^2 - 2z + 5\right)$

9. The graphs of $f(x) = x^3$ and $g(x) = (x + 2)^3$ are shown.

   a. How many zeros does each function have?

   b. Describe the transformation of *f* represented by *g*.

   c. Determine the intervals for which the function *g* is increasing or decreasing.

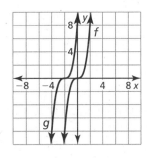

10. The volume *V* (in cubic feet) of a shipping box is modeled by the polynomial function $V(x) = x^3 - 2x^2 - 19x + 20$, where *x* is the length of the box.

   a. Explain how you know $x = -2$ is *not* a possible rational zero.

   b. Show that $x + 4$ is a factor of $V(x)$. Then factor $V(x)$ completely.

Answers

1. _____

2. _____

3. _____

4. _____

5. _____

6. _____

7. _____

8. _____

9. a._____

   _____

   b._____

   _____

   c._____

   _____

10. a.___See left.___

    b.___See left.___

Chapter 4 Test A (continued)

11. Let F be the number (in millions) of new football jersey sales. Let B be the number (in millions) of new baseball jersey sales. During a 5-year period, F and B can be modeled by the following equations, where t represents the time (in years).

$$F = 12t^4 - 20t^3 - 20t + 900$$
$$B = 15t^4 - 10t^3 + 10t^2 - 30t + 700$$

   a. Find a new model A for the total number of new football and baseball jersey sales.

   b. Is the function A *even*, *odd*, or *neither*? Explain your reasoning.

12. You have decided to start a dog-walking business. The table below shows the profits p (in dollars) of the business during your first 6 years. Use a graphing calculator and finite differences to find a polynomial model for the problem. Then use the model to predict your profit after 10 years.

Year, t	1	2	3	4	5	6
Profit, p	7	11	23	49	95	167

13. The graph of a cubic function $f(x)$ is shown. Describe the degree and leading coefficient of f.

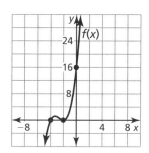

14. The function $V(x) = \frac{4}{3}\pi x^3$ represents the volume (in cubic feet) of a sphere with a radius of x feet shown. The function $W(x) = V(12x)$ represents this volume in cubic inches. Write a rule for W. Find $W(5)$.

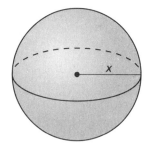

Answers

11. a._____

    b._____

    _____

    _____

12. _____

    _____

13. _____

    _____

14. _____

    _____

Name_____ Date_____

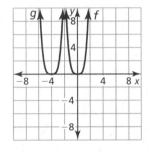

Chapter 4 Test B

Write a polynomial function f of least degree that has rational coefficients, a leading coefficient of 1, and the given zeros.

Answers

1. $-2, -1, -i$

2. $4, -\sqrt{5}, -5$

Find the product or quotient.

3. $(2x - 2)^2$

4. $(c^8 - 6)(c^2 - 4c - 2)$

5. $(4x^3 + 20x^2 + 12x - 16) \div (x - 4)$

6. $(b + 3)(b + 3)(b + 2)$

7. $(3x^4 - 2x^3 + 5x - 3) \div (x^2 - 3x + 1)$

8. $(3x + 1)^3$

9. The graphs of $f(x) = x^4$ and $g(x) = (x + 4)^4$ are shown.

    a. How many zeros does each function have?

    b. Describe the transformation of f represented by g.

    c. Determine the intervals for which the function g is increasing or decreasing.

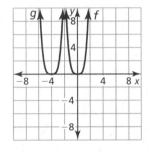

1. _____

2. _____

3. _____

4. _____

5. _____

6. _____

7. _____

8. _____

9. a._____

_____

b._____

_____

c._____

_____

10. a.__See left.__

b.__See left.__

10. The volume V (in cubic feet) of a hot tub is modeled by the polynomial function $V(x) = x^3 - 10x^2 + 11x + 70$, where x is the length of the hot tub.

    a. Explain how you know $x = -5$ is *not* a possible rational zero.

    b. Show that $x + 2$ is a factor of $V(x)$. Then factor $V(x)$ completely.

Chapter 4 Test B (continued)

11. Your student council decided to start a pencil sale. The table below shows the profits p of the sale during the first 5 months. Use a graphing calculator and finite differences to find a polynomial model for the problem. Then use the model to predict the profit after 12 months.

Month, t	1	2	3	4	5
Profit, p	1	4	23	70	157

Answers

11. _____

_____

12. _____

_____

12. The graph of a cubic function $f(x)$ is shown. Describe the degree and the leading coefficient of f.

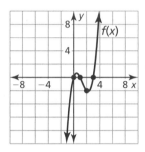

13. a._____

   b._____

   _____

   _____

14. _____

_____

13. Let G be the number (in billions) of new green tea sales. Let J be the number (in billions) of new fruit juice sales. During a 20-year period, G and J can be modeled by the following equation, where t is the time (in years).

$$G = 6t^4 + 3t^3 - 2t^2 + 5t + 60$$
$$J = 3t^4 - 3t^3 + 5t^2 - 5t + 45$$

   a. Find a new model A for the total number of new green tea and fruit juice sales.

   b. Is the new function A *even*, *odd*, or *neither*? Explain your reasoning.

14. The function $V(x) = 27x^2 - 9x$ represents the volume (in cubic yards) of a cylinder shown. The function $W(x) = V\left(\frac{1}{3}x\right)$ represents the volume in cubic feet, when x is measured in yards. Write a rule for W. Find $W(15)$.

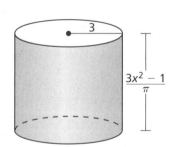

Chapter 4 Alternative Assessment

1. Consider the product of two binomials. For the following, show your multiplication to verify the product is a polynomial of the type specified.

   a. Find two binomials whose product is also a binomial.

   b. Find two binomials whose product is a trinomial.

   c. Find two binomials whose product is a polynomial with four terms.

2. Consider the binomial $x^6 - y^6$.

   a. Factor this completely as the difference of two squares.

   b. Factor this completely as the difference of two cubes.

   c. Use parts (a) and (b) to show that
   $\left(x^2 + xy + y^2\right)\left(x^2 - xy + y^2\right) = x^4 + x^2y^2 + y^4$. Verify this with polynomial multiplication.

3. Find three consecutive positive integers whose product is 336 using the following methods.

   a. Write three different ways to represent the product of the integers. (*Hint:* Let x equal the first number in one case, the second number in another, and the third in another.)

   b. For each representation, write an equation in standard form showing that the product is 336.

   c. Solve each equation graphically. Verify that each representation yields the same set of three integers.

   d. Besides solving a polynomial equation, what other methods could you use to find the integers?

Name _____ Date _____

Score	Conceptual Understanding	Mathematical Skills	Work Habits
4	Shows complete understanding of: • Multiplying polynomials • Factoring polynomials completely	Binomials listed in Exercise 1 satisfy all conditions The factorization in Exercise 2 is correct and complete. Three correct representations and equations are shown in Exercise 3.	Answers all parts of all problems The answers are explained thoroughly with mathematical terminology. Work is very neat and well organized.
3	Shows nearly complete understanding of: • Multiplying polynomials • Factoring polynomials completely	Binomials listed in Exercise 1 satisfy two conditions The factorization in Exercise 2 is correct, but not complete for one method. Three correct representations and equations are shown in Exercise 3.	Answers most parts of all problems The answers are explained with mathematical terminology. Work is neat and organized.
2	Shows some understanding of: • Multiplying polynomials • Factoring polynomials completely	Binomials listed in Exercise 1 satisfy one condition The factorization in Exercise 2 is correct, but not complete for either method. Three representations are correct, but the equation in standard form is missing from Exercise 3.	Answers some parts of all problems The answers are poorly or incorrectly explained. Work is not very neat or organized.
1	Shows little understanding of: • Multiplying polynomials • Factoring polynomials completely	No binomials listed in Exercise 1 are correct The factorization in Exercise 2 is incorrect. One representation is incorrect or missing from Exercise 3.	Attempts few parts of any problem No explanation is included with the answers. Work is sloppy and disorganized.

Name_____ Date _____

 Performance Task

For the Birds—Wildlife Management

Instructional Overview	
Launch Question	How does the presence of humans affect the population of sparrows in a park? Do more humans mean fewer sparrows? Or does the presence of humans increase the number of sparrows up to a point? Are there a minimum number of sparrows that can be found in a park, regardless of how many humans are there? What can a mathematical model tell you?
Summary	Students will compare equations from different polynomial regression models (linear, quadratic, and cubic) calculated from the same data set. They will examine the data set to observe which data points affect the chosen regression the most.
Teacher Notes	This data comes from an actual study of how an urban landscape affects sparrow density, *Testing the Risk-Disturbance Hypothesis in a Fragmented Landscape: Nonlinear Responses of House Sparrows to Humans*. The study was done by Esteban Fernandez-Juricic, Angel Sallent, Ruben Sanz, and Inaki Rodriguez-Prieto from the University of Minnesota and was published in the journal of the Cooper Ornithological Society, *The Condor*, vol. 105, pp. 316–326 (2003).
	The article includes data from two different years. The full data set and article can be found at the website below.
	http://estebanfj.bio.purdue.edu/papers/Condor105.pdf
	This would be a good activity to do in pairs to encourage discussion and exchange ideas and questions.
Supplies	Calculators
Mathematical Discourse	If a relationship between two things or a physical phenomenon is best modeled by a linear function, what are some conclusions you can draw about that relationship? How about a quadratic function? A cubic function?
Writing/Discussion Prompts	1. Discuss how outliers affected this data set. How should they be treated and analyzed?
	2. What could explain why a population increases, decreases, and then increases again?

Chapter 4 Performance Task (continued)

For the Birds—Wildlife Management

Curriculum Content	
CCSSM Content Standards	HSF-IF.1, HSF-IF.2, HSF-IF.4, HSF-IF.5, HSA-CED.1, HSA-CED.1, HSF-LE.1
CCSSM Mathematical Practices	3. Construct viable arguments and critique the reasoning of others: There are many possible factors that could contribute to the change in sparrow population. Students must explore and explain more than one factor as well as understand the arguments of others. 4. Model with mathematics: Students apply three polynomial regressions to the same data set.

Rubric

For the Birds—Wildlife Management	Points
1. and 6. 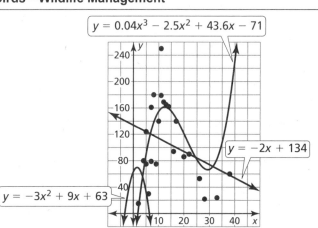 $y = 0.04x^3 - 2.5x^2 + 43.6x - 71$ $y = -2x + 134$ $y = -3x^2 + 9x + 63$ 1. *Sample answer:* domain: $0 \le x \le 40$, between 0 and 40 people per hectare; range: $0 \le y \le 250$, between 0 and 250 birds per hectare 2. no; The numbers 5, 7, and 11 repeat in the domain; Repeated x-values show that different parks might have the same density of people.	**3** All correct **2** One graph incorrect or domain incorrect **1** One or more graphs incorrect and domain incorrect

3. *Sample answer:* For smaller populations of humans, the bird population appears to increase with the human population. However, beyond about 10 people per hectare, the bird population begins to decrease as the human population increases.
 4. a. $y = -2x + 134$; $r^2 = 0.09$
    b. $y = -0.3x^2 + 9x + 63.7$; $r^2 = 0.3$
    c. $y = 0.04x^3 - 2.5x^2 + 43.6x - 71$; $r^2 = 0.63$
	5 All answers correct
	 3 One model incorrect
	 1 Two or more models incorrect

Chapter 4 **Performance Task** (continued)

Rubric (continued)

For the Birds—Wildlife Management	Points

5. cubic; $r^2 = 0.63$ indicates a better fit than 0.3 or 0.09.
 	
7. a. 134, the number of sparrows when no humans are present
  b. 67; the number of humans for which there are no sparrows
  c. sparrows decrease by 2 for each increase of 1 human
  d. sparrows only decrease; does not take initial increase into account
 	
8. a. 63.7; the number of sparrows when no humans are present
  b. 36; the number of humans for which there are no sparrows
  c. (15, 131.2); The largest number of sparrows occurs at about 15 people per hectare.
  d. models increase followed by decrease better than linear model; sparrows never increase again
 	
9. a. −71; the number of sparrows when no humans are present
  b. 1.8; near origin, model suggests there are no sparrows unless there are at least 2 humans
  c. maximum (12.4, 161.5); minimum (29.2, 66.4); maximum bird population is about 162, for about 12 people per hectare; minimum bird population is about 66, for about 29 people per hectare
  d. fits data shape better than linear or quadratic; sparrow population increases forever
 	
10. *Sample answer:* A cubic model would imply the population would increase forever. That is not realistic because at some point there will not be enough space to breed even though the humans may be providing food; Make sure each student chooses a preferred model and provides reasoning. *Sample answer:* linear model; It is easier to calculate; cubic model; r^2 shows best fit for this model.
	7 All answers correct
	5 Most answers correct
	3 Some answers correct
	1 Few answers correct

Mathematics Practice: Construct viable arguments. Reasoning should be sound, thorough, and well explained.	**3** For demonstration of practice; Partial credit can be awarded.
Total Points	**18 points**

Chapter 4 Performance Task (continued)

For the Birds—Wildlife Management

How does the presence of humans affect the population of sparrows in a park? Do more humans mean fewer sparrows? Or does the presence of humans increase the number of sparrows up to a point? Are there a minimum number of sparrows that can be found in a park, regardless of how many humans are there? What can a mathematical model tell you?

In 1997, researchers set out to answer these questions. They observed the sparrow population and the numbers of pedestrians in wooded parks. Their approximate data can be seen below.

Number of pedestrians per hectare	2	4	5	5	6	7	7	8	9	10	11
Number of sparrows per hectare	15	80	75	124	30	79	161	180	75	140	179

Number of pedestrians per hectare	11	12	13	14	16	17	20	22	26	28	33	38
Number of sparrows per hectare	250	169	165	162	94	140	86	90	53	22	24	60

1. Make a scatter plot of the data. Explain your domain and range.

2. Does the data represent a function? Why or why not? What might explain the duplicate entries?

3. What trends do you see in the data?

4. Using the regression feature of your calculator, find three models for this data along with the corresponding coefficients of determination.

   a. a linear model

   b. a quadratic model

   c. a cubic model

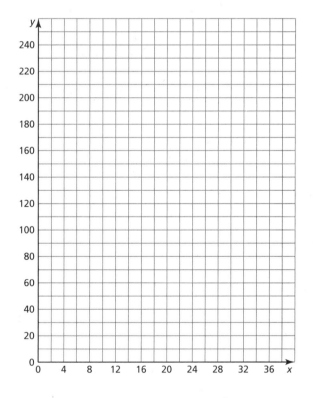

Performance Task (continued)

5. According to the coefficient of determination, which model fits the data best? Why?

6. Graph the three regression equations with your scatter plot.

7. Focusing on the linear model:

    a. What is the *y*-intercept, and what does it represent?

    b. What is the *x*-intercept, and what does it represent?

    c. Interpret the slope of the model with respect to the data.

    d. What is realistic about this model? What is unrealistic?

Chapter 4 **Performance Task** (continued)

8. Focusing on the quadratic model:

   a. What is the *y*-intercept, and what does it represent?

   b. What is the *x*-intercept, and what does it represent?

   c. What is the maximum point of the model? What does it represent?

   d. What is realistic about this model? What is unrealistic?

9. Focusing on the cubic model:

   a. What is the *y*-intercept, and what does it represent?

   b. What is the *x*-intercept, and what does it represent?

   c. What is the relative maximum point of the model? What is the relative minimum of the model? What do they represent?

   d. What is realistic about this model? What is unrealistic?

10. Why do you think the researchers for this study chose a quadratic model for their data even though the coefficient of determination for this model was not the highest? Which model would you have chosen? Explain your reasoning.

Name_____ Date _____

Teacher Notes:

Name _____ Date _____

Find the indicated real *n*th root(s) of *a*.

Answers

1. $n = 4, a = 16$

2. $n = 3, a = -125$

1. _____

3. Evaluate (a) $25^{3/2}$ and (b) $256^{3/4}$ without using a calculator.

2. _____

Find the real solution(s) of the equation. Round your answer to two decimal places.

3. a. _____

   b. _____

4. $3x^5 = 3072$

5. $(x + 5)^3 = 50$

4. _____

Simplify the expression.

5. _____

6. $\left(\dfrac{72^{1/5}}{9^{1/5}}\right)^3$

7. $\sqrt[3]{2} \cdot \sqrt[3]{250}$

8. $\dfrac{1}{8 - \sqrt{2}}$

6. _____

7. _____

Write the expression in simplest form. Assume all variables are positive.

8. _____

9. $\sqrt[4]{625m^{10}}$

10. $\dfrac{\sqrt[4]{81}}{\sqrt[3]{x^2}}$

11. $7\sqrt[5]{b^5 n} - 2b\sqrt[10]{n^2}$

9. _____

10. _____

Describe the transformation of the parent function represented by the graph of *g*. Then write a rule for *g*.

11. _____

12.
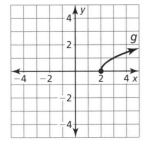

13.
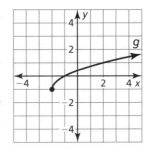

12. _____

_____

13. _____

_____

14. Use a graphing calculator to graph $x = 5y^2 + 2$. Identify the vertex and direction the parabola opens.

14. _____

_____

15. A cylindrical container of water has a volume of 190 cubic inches. The radius *r* of the container can be found by using the formula $r = \sqrt{\dfrac{V}{\pi h}}$, where *V* is the volume of the container and *h* is the height.

15. a. _____

   b. _____

   a. If the radius of the container is 3.5 inches, find the height. Round your answer to the nearest hundredth.

   b. If the height of the container is 10 inches, find the radius. Round your answer to the nearest hundredth.

Name_____ Date _____

Chapter 5 Test A

Simplify the expression.

Answers

1. $8^{4/3}$

2. $\dfrac{\sqrt[4]{208}}{\sqrt[4]{13}}$

3. $\sqrt[5]{32xy^6z^5}$

4. $(-125)^{2/3}$

5. $12\sqrt{5} - 2\sqrt{125}$

6. $\dfrac{1}{1 + \sqrt{3}}$

1. _____

2. _____

3. _____

4. _____

5. _____

6. _____

7. _____

8. _____

9. _____

10. _____

11. _____

12. _____

The transformation of *f* is represented by *g*. Write a rule for *g*.

7. $f(x) = \sqrt{x}$

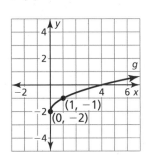

8. $f(x) = \sqrt[3]{x}$

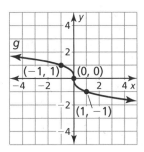

9. $f(x) = \sqrt[5]{x}$

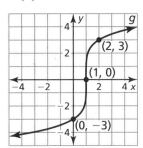

10. $f(x) = \sqrt{x}$

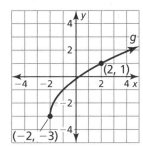

11. The speed of a vehicle just before the brakes are applied can be estimated by using the formula $s = (28.75d)^{1/2}$, where *s* is the speed (in miles per hour) of the vehicle and *d* is the length (in feet) of the skid marks the vehicle leaves. How fast was a car traveling if it left skid marks 45 feet long? Round your answer to the nearest hundredth.

12. Let $f(x) = 3x^{5/3}$ and $g(x) = -2x^{5/3}$. Find $(f + g)(x)$ and $(f - g)(x)$ and state the domain of each. Then evaluate $(f + g)(-8)$ and $(f - g)(-8)$.

13. Let $f(x) = \frac{1}{2}x^{5/2}$ and $g(x) = 2x^2$. Find $(f \bullet g)(x)$ and $\left(\dfrac{f}{g}\right)(x)$ and state

the domain of each. Then evaluate $(f \bullet g)(9)$ and $\left(\dfrac{f}{g}\right)(9)$.

13. _____

Chapter 5 **Test A** (continued)

14. Solve the inequality $4\sqrt{x + 3} + 3 \leq 15$ and the equation $4\sqrt{x + 3} + 3 = 15$. Describe a similarity and a difference between solving radical equations and inequalities.

15. Write two functions whose graphs are translations of the graph $y = \sqrt{x}$. The first function should have a domain of $x \geq 2$. The second function should have a range of $y \geq -1$.

16. The function $h(w) = 6.5\sqrt[3]{w}$ models the height h (in inches) using the weight w of many small female animals. Use the table to find the height of each of the given animals. Record your answers in the table. Round your answers to the nearest tenth.

Female animal	Weight	Height
robin	3 ounces	
rabbit	30 ounces	
red squirrel	11 ounces	
hamster	4 ounces	

17. The average speed that a tsunami (a large tidal wave) travels is represented by the function $s = (200d)^{1/2}$, where s is the speed (in miles per hour) that the tsunami is traveling and d is the average depth (in feet) of the wave.

    a. Find the inverse of the function.

    b. Find the average depth of the tsunami when the recorded speed of the wave is 250 miles per hour.

Answers

14. ___See left.___

15. _____

    _____

16. ___See left.___

17. a._____

    b._____

Name_____ Date _____

Simplify the expression.

1. $(-32)^{3/5}$

2. $2\sqrt{72} - 3\sqrt{2}$

3. $\dfrac{\sqrt[5]{1215}}{\sqrt[5]{5}}$

4. $\sqrt[3]{-8x^3y^5z^7}$

5. $27^{2/3}$

6. $\dfrac{2}{1 - \sqrt{2}}$

The transformation of *f* is represented by *g*. Write a rule for *g*.

7. $f(x) = \sqrt{x}$

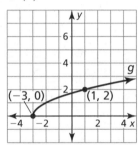

8. $f(x) = \sqrt[3]{x}$

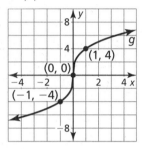

9. $f(x) = \sqrt[5]{x}$

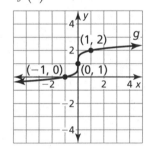

10. $f(x) = \sqrt{x}$

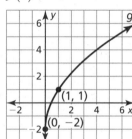

11. At the circus, the length of time *t* (in seconds) it takes for a trapeze artist to complete one full walk is given by the equation $t = 2.31\ell^{1/2}$, where ℓ is the length (in feet) of the trapeze line. The table below shows the length of the lines a certain performer must walk each show. How long will each walk take? Round your answers to the nearest tenth.

Act	Walk length	Time
Act 1	60 feet	
Act 2	40 feet	
Act 3	100 feet	
Act 4	300 feet	

12. Let $f(x) = -2x^{2/5}$ and $g(x) = -x^{2/5}$. Find $(f + g)(x)$ and $(f - g)(x)$ and state the domain of each. Then evaluate $(f + g)(243)$ and $(f - g)(243)$.

Answers

1. _____

2. _____

3. _____

4. _____

5. _____

6. _____

7. _____

8. _____

9. _____

10. _____

11. ___**See left.**___

12. _____

_____

_____

_____

_____

_____

_____

_____

Test B (continued)

Answers

13. Let $f(x) = \dfrac{2}{3}x^{3/2}$ and $g(x) = -4x$. Find $(f \bullet g)(x)$ and $\left(\dfrac{f}{g}\right)(x)$ and state

    the domain of each. Then evaluate $(f \bullet g)(4)$ and $\left(\dfrac{f}{g}\right)(4)$.

14. Write two functions whose graphs are translations of the graph $y = \sqrt{x}$.
    The first function should have a domain of $x \geq -3$. The second function
    should have a range of $y \leq 3$.

15. The equation $d = (1.35h)^{1/2}$ represents the distance d (in feet) you can see
    out into the horizon, where h is the height (in feet) of your eyes above
    ground level. Determine how tall a person is if he or she can see 2.75 miles
    out into the horizon. Round your answer to the nearest hundredth.

16. Solve the inequality $6\sqrt{x-2} + 4 \leq 28$ and the equation
    $6\sqrt{x-2} + 4 = 28$. Describe a similarity and a difference between solving
    radical equations and inequalities.

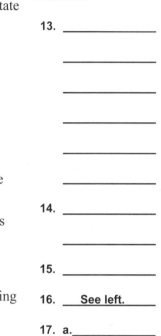

13. _____

    _____

    _____

    _____

    _____

    _____

14. _____

    _____

15. _____

16. ___See left.___

17. a._____

    b._____

17. The total number of months m that it takes to produce p tennis rackets
    (in thousands) is given by the formula $m = \dfrac{p^3}{90}$.

    a. Find the inverse of the function.

    b. How many tennis rackets will be produced in 20 months? Round your
       answer to the nearest whole tennis racket.

Chapter 5 Alternative Assessment

1. Which of the following expressions are equal to 4?

   a. $\left(\sqrt[4]{16}\right)^2$

   b. $\sqrt{4} + \sqrt[3]{8}$

   c. $2\sqrt[5]{32}$

   d. $4^0 \cdot 4^1$

   e. $64^{1/3}$

   f. $\sqrt[3]{2} \cdot \sqrt[3]{4} \cdot \sqrt[3]{8}$

2. Your local recreation center is trying to encourage more teens to attend its open pool events. The center has asked your school to design a diving dock that could be used in the deep end. You are leading this effort, and your team has proposed a dock with the main landing in the shape of a rectangle with two square diving platforms centered on two sides. The length and width of the main landing are three times and two times the side length of the diving platforms, respectively.

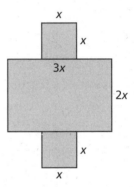

   a. Write a function A_1 for the area of the main landing. Write a function A_2 for the area of a diving platform.

   b. Write a function A for the area of the entire diving dock.

   c. Graph the function A. How can you use the graph to explain why the inverse of A is not a function?

   d. How can you restrict the domain of A so that A^{-1} is a function? Why does this restriction make sense in the context of the problem?

   e. Solve the function A for x, assuming that the domain of A is restricted as described in part (d). What information can you obtain?

   f. You have 200 square feet of material to make the dock. Use the function solved for x from part (e) to find the dimensions of the main landing and of each diving platform.

Chapter 5 Alternative Assessment Rubric

Score	Conceptual Understanding	Mathematical Skills	Work Habits
4	Shows complete understanding of: • rational exponents • function operations • inverse of a function	List all expressions as correct answers to Exercise 1 All functions, including the inverse, in Exercise 2 are correct. The radical is simplified correctly. The correct dimensions are calculated for Exercise 3. All explanations are correct.	Answers all parts of all problems The answers are explained thoroughly with mathematical terminology. Work is very neat and well organized.
3	Shows nearly complete understanding of: • rational exponents • function operations • inverse of a function	One expression is omitted in Exercise 1. One function in Exercise 2 is incorrect. One explanation is omitted or incorrect.	Answers most parts of all problems The answers are explained with mathematical terminology. Work is neat and organized.
2	Shows some understanding of: • rational exponents • function operations • inverse of a function	Two expressions are omitted in Exercise 1. Two functions in Exercise 2 are incorrect. Neither explanation is correct, but both were attempted.	Answers some parts of all problems The answers are poorly or incorrectly explained. Work is not very neat or organized.
1	Shows little understanding of: • rational exponents • function operations • inverse of a function	More than two expressions are omitted in Exercise 1. More than two functions in Exercise 2 are incorrect. Neither explanation was attempted.	Attempts few parts of any problem No explanation is included with the answers. Work is sloppy and disorganized.

Name_____ Date_____

Chapter 5 Performance Task

Turning the Tables

Instructional Overview	
Launch Question	In this chapter, you have used properties of rational exponents and functions to find an answer to the problem. Using those same properties, can you find a problem to the answer? How many problems can you find?
Summary	Students will decompose rational expressions using properties of exponents.
Teacher Notes	This task can be extended into so many engaging activities. It can be the basis of a competition in which teams are challenged to come up with the most unique representations of a given expression. A twist on this would be to challenge students to write one equivalent representation that requires all exponent rules. Similarly, a card/dice game could be made in which an expression card is drawn, a rule die is rolled, and players are challenged to find an equivalent expression using the specified rule. The possibilities are endless! Have fun!
Supplies	Handouts
Mathematical Discourse	1. What is the difference between integer exponents and rational exponents?
Writing/Discussion Prompts	1. Use the Quotient Property of Exponents to verify that any number raised to the 0 power is 1.

Curriculum Content	
CCSSM Content Standards	HSN-RN.1, HSN-RN.2, HSN-RN.3, HSA-SSE.2, HSA-APR.6
CCSSM Mathematical Practices	2. Reason abstractly and quantitatively: Students must reverse the usual process of solving a problem to create a problem. 7. Look for and make use of structure: Students must rewrite exponents as sums, differences, and powers.

Performance Task (continued)

Rubric

Turning the Tables	Points
Students understand multiplication of rational exponents. *Sample answers:* 1. a. $8^{1/18} \bullet 8^{1/6}$, b. $\left(8^{1/9}\right)^2$, c. $\left(8^{3/2} \bullet 8^{1/2}\right)^{1/9}$ 2. a. $\dfrac{x^3 \bullet x^1}{y \bullet y}$, b. $\left(\dfrac{x^2}{y}\right)^2$, c. $\left(x^8 \bullet \dfrac{1}{y^4}\right)^{1/2}$ 3. a. $\dfrac{64}{81}z^2 \bullet z^2 \bullet z^2$, b. $\dfrac{64}{81}\left(z^2\right)^3$, c. $\left(\dfrac{8}{9} \bullet z^3\right)^2$	**7** All correct **5** Most correct **3** Some correct **2** Few correct
Students understand zero and negative exponents. *Sample answers:* 1. d. $\dfrac{1}{8^{-2/9}}$, e. $8^{2/9} \bullet (829)^0$ 2. d. $\dfrac{y^{-2}}{x^{-4}}$, e. $\dfrac{x^3 \bullet x^1 \bullet x^0}{y^1 \bullet y^0 \bullet y^1}$ 3. d. $\left(\dfrac{81}{64z^6}\right)^{-1}$, e. $\dfrac{81x^3 \bullet x^2 \bullet x^1 \bullet x^0}{64}$	**5** All correct **3** Most correct **1** Few correct
Students understand multiplication of rational exponents. *Sample answers:* 1. f. $\dfrac{8^{3/9}}{8^{1/9}}$, g. $\left(\dfrac{1}{8^{1/9}}\right)^{-2}$ 2. f. $\dfrac{x^6 \bullet y^1}{x^2 \bullet y^3}$, g. $\left(\dfrac{y^2}{x^4}\right)^{-1}$ 3. f. $\dfrac{8^3 \bullet 9^2 \bullet z^7}{8 \bullet 9^4 \bullet z}$, g. $\left(\dfrac{8z^3}{9}\right)^2$	**5** All correct **3** Most correct **1** Few correct
Mathematics Practice: Reason abstractly and quantitatively.	**3** For demonstration of practice; Partial credit can be awarded.
Total Points	**20 points**

Chapter 5 **Performance Task** (continued)

Turning the Tables

In this chapter, you have used properties of rational exponents and functions to find an answer to the problem. Using those same properties, can you find a problem to the answer? How many problems can you find?

For each answer, create an equivalent expression that requires the specified property of exponents to simplify.

Answer 1: $8^{2/9}$

Answer 2: $\dfrac{x^4}{y^2}$

Answer 3: $\dfrac{64z^6}{81}$

    a. Product of Powers

    b. Power of a Power

    c. Power of a Product

    d. Negative Exponent

    e. Zero Exponent

    f. Quotient of Powers

    g. Power of a Quotient

Name _____ Date _____

Tell whether the function represents *exponential growth* **or** *exponential decay*. **Explain your reasoning.**

Answers

1. $f(x) = (1.75)^x$ **2.** $f(x) = 3e^{-x}$

Simplify the expression.

3. $\dfrac{24e^5}{6e}$ **4.** $\left(3e^{2x}\right)^3$

5. $e^{\ln 5}$ **6.** $\log_4 64^{-3x}$

Rewrite the expression in exponential or logarithmic form.

7. $\log_3 243 = 5$ **8.** $2^{-3} = 0.125$

Evaluate the logarithm. If necessary, use a calculator and round your answer to three decimal places.

9. $\log 35$ **10.** $\ln 1.8$ **11.** $\log_4 256$

Graph the function and its inverse.

12. $f(x) = 4^x$

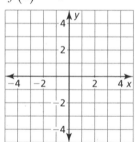

13. $f(x) = \log_3(x - 2)$

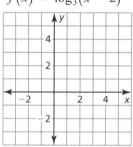

The graph of *g* **is a transformation of the graph of** *f*. **Write a rule for** *g*.

14. $f(x) = \log_2 x$

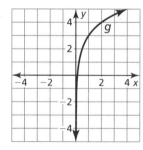

15. $f(x) = 4^x$

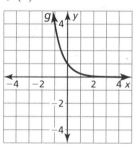

16. You purchased a baseball card for $8 when you were 10 years old. The value of the card increased by 5% each year. Write an exponential model that gives the value *y* (in dollars) of the card *t* years after you purchased it.

Answers	
1.	_____
	_____
2.	_____
	_____
3.	_____
4.	_____
5.	_____
6.	_____
7.	_____
8.	_____
9.	_____
10.	_____
11.	_____
12.	_See left._
13.	_See left._
14.	_____
15.	_____
16.	_____

80 **Algebra 2**
Assessment Book

Name_____ Date_____

Graph the equation.   *Answers*

1. $y = \left(\frac{1}{4}\right)^x$ 2. $y = \log_2 x$ 3. $y = -\frac{1}{2}e^{-x}$ 1. ___See left.___

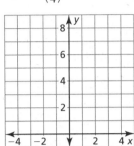   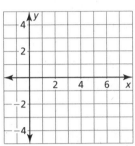   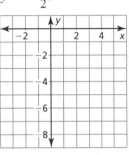

2. ___See left.___

3. ___See left.___

4. _____

5. _____

6. _____

Evaluate the logarithm. Use $\log_2 5 \approx 2.3219$ **and** $\log_2 7 \approx 2.8074$,   7. _____

if necessary.   8. _____

4. $\log_2 \frac{7}{5}$ 5. $\log_2 35$ 6. $\log_2 25 + \log_2 \frac{1}{5}$ 9. _____

7. $\log_2 63 - \log_2 9$ 8. $\log_2 3 + \log_2 15 - \log_2 9$

10. _____

Describe the transformation of *f* **represented by** *g***. Then write a rule for** *g***.**

9. $f(x) = \log x$ 10. $f(x) = e^x$ 11. _____

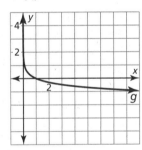   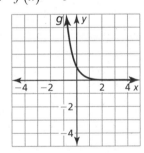

12. _____

13. _____

11. $f(x) = \left(\frac{1}{2}\right)^x$ 12. $f(x) = e^x$

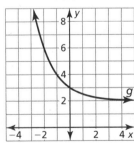   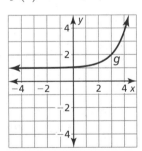

13. Without calculating, determine whether $\log_3 7$, $\dfrac{\log 7}{\log 3}$, and $\dfrac{\ln 7}{\ln 3}$ are equivalent.

Chapter 6 Test A (continued)

Solve the equation.

14. $3^{2x-3} = 27$

15. $\log_3(4x - 7) = 2$

16. $25^x = \left(\frac{1}{5}\right)^{x-3}$

17. $\ln(2x + 3) = \ln(5x - 6)$

18. The average number of free throws a basketball player can make consecutively during practice is modeled by the function $f(x) = 1 + 1.3 \ln(x + 1)$, where x is the number of consecutive days the player has practiced for 1 hour. After how many days of practice can the basketball player make an average of five consecutive free throws? Round your answer to the nearest whole number of days.

19. The function $P = 18e^{kt}$ models the population (in millions) of a particular country t years after 2013.

a. A recent change in the economy has made the k-value, or rate of change in population, 0.231. Write a function that gives the population of the country using this k-value.

b. Tell whether your function in part (a) represents exponential growth or exponential decay.

c. Estimate the population of this country in 2023. Round your answer to the nearest million.

20. The table shows the values (in thousands) of the average salary of NBA players x years after 1990. Write and use an exponential model to find the year when the average NBA player's salary will be more than $4 million.

Years (after 1990), x	1	2	3	4	5	6	7
Salary (thousands), y	25	50	100	200	400	800	1600

Answers

14. _____

15. _____

16. _____

17. _____

18. _____

19. a._____

   b._____

   c._____

20. _____

   _____

Chapter 6 **Test B**

Graph the equation.   *Answers*

1. $y = \left(\dfrac{1}{3}\right)^x$ **2.** $y = \log_{1/2} x$ **3.** $y = 2e^{3x}$

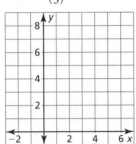   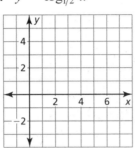   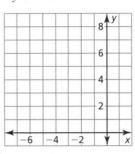

Evaluate the logarithm. Use log₄ 5 ≈ 1.1610 and log₄ 11 ≈ 1.7297, if necessary.

4. $\log_4 55$ **5.** $\log_4 \dfrac{11}{5}$ **6.** $\log_4 121$

7. $\log_4 22 - \log_4 \dfrac{1}{2}$ **8.** $\log_4 6 + \log_4 10 - \log_4 12$

Describe the transformation of *f* represented by *g*. Then write a rule for *g*.

9. $f(x) = \log x$ **10.** $f(x) = e^x$

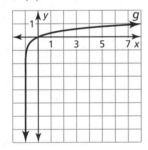   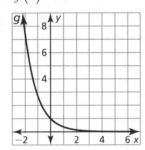

11. $f(x) = \left(\dfrac{1}{2}\right)^x$ **12.** $f(x) = e^x$

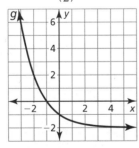   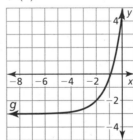

13. Without calculating, determine whether $\log_6 13$, $\dfrac{\log 13}{\log 6}$, and $\dfrac{\ln 13}{\ln 6}$ are equivalent.

Answers

1.   See left.

2.   See left.

3.   See left.

4. _____

5. _____

6. _____

7. _____

8. _____

9. _____

10. _____

_____

11. _____

_____

12. _____

_____

13. _____

Solve the equation.   *Answers*

14. $2^{2x-1} = 8$ **15.** $\log_2(7x + 9) = 1$

16. $9^x = \left(\dfrac{1}{3}\right)^{2x-4}$ **17.** $\ln(2x + 5) = \ln(3x - 3)$

18. The number of new chain saws sold t years after the introduction of a new model is given by the function $y = 2300\ln(8t + 3)$. How many chain saws will be sold 5 years after the new model is introduced? Round your answer to the nearest whole number.

19. An endangered species of bird has a population that is modeled by the exponential equation $A = 1600e^{kt}$, where A (in hundreds) represents the current population of the birds t years from now.

   a. Scientists recently discovered the k-value, or rate of the bird population change, to be -0.23. Write a function that gives the current population.

   b. Tell whether your function in part (a) represents exponential growth or exponential decay.

   c. What will the population be 6 years from now?

20. The table shows the number of rabbits r in a particular forest t years after a forest fire. Write and use an exponential model to find how many years it will take for the rabbit population to surpass 20,000.

Years after fire, y	0	1	2	3	4	5
Rabbits, r	20	60	180	540	1620	4860

Answers:
14. _____
15. _____
16. _____
17. _____
18. _____
19. a. _____
b. _____
c. _____
20. _____
_____

Name_____ Date _____

1. In 2000, a home builder builds the exact same model of a house in two different cities in two different states. The table shows the value of each house, v_1 and v_2, for t years after 2000.

Time (years), t	2	4	6	8	10
Value, v_1 (thousands of dollars)	360	367	373	381	387
Value, v_2 (thousands of dollars)	310	350	400	461	520

   a. Analyze the growth in home values using your knowledge about finite differences and common ratios. What are your conclusions?

   b. Based on your result in part (a), what types of functions will best model each set of data?

   c. Find a model for the value of each house.

   d. Using your models, estimate the value of each house in 2021.

   e. Approximately how many years would it take the value of the first house, v_1, to reach $500,000? Determine the solution algebraically.

   f. In what year were the values of the two houses equal? Describe how you can find this solution graphically and algebraically. What method will you choose to find your answer and why?

   g. Describe the rate of change in the value of each house. What factors may have affected the values of the two houses?

Name _____ Date _____

Score	Conceptual Understanding	Mathematical Skills	Work Habits
4	Shows complete understanding of: • identifying an exponential function • modeling with exponential regression • solving a system of equations including an exponential function	The models for both value functions are correctly defined and used to predict values.	Answers all parts of all problems The answers are explained with mathematical terminology. Work is very neat and well organized.
3	Shows nearly complete understanding of: • identifying an exponential function • modeling with exponential regression • solving a system of equations including an exponential function	The models for both functions are defined correctly, but at least one of the predicted values is incorrect.	Answers most parts of all problems The answers are explained with mathematical terminology. Work is neat and organized.
2	Shows some understanding of: • identifying an exponential function • modeling with exponential regression • solving a system of equations including an exponential function	At least one model is defined incorrectly.	Answers some parts of all problems The answers are poorly or incorrectly explained. Work is not very neat or organized.
1	Shows little understanding of: • identifying an exponential function • modeling with exponential regression • solving a system of equations including an exponential function	Both models are defined incorrectly.	Attempts few parts of any problem No explanation is included with the answers. Work is sloppy and disorganized.

Name_____ Date_____

Performance Task

Measuring Natural Disasters

Instructional Overview	
Launch Question	In 2005, an earthquake measuring 4.1 on the Richter scale barely shook the city of Ocotillo, California, leaving virtually no damage. But in 1906, an earthquake with an estimated 8.2 on the same scale devastated the city of San Francisco. Does twice the measurement on the Richter scale mean twice the intensity of the earthquake?
Summary	Students will interpret log scales.
Teacher Notes	Students may be surprised to learn that earthquakes happen every day all over the United States. Humans cannot even feel a microquake, defined as having a magnitude of 2 or less, and small quakes in the range of 2.5 to 5.4 are often felt as a small rumble but only cause minor damage if any at all. Strong (6–6.9), major (7–7.9), and great (8 or higher) quakes are responsible for loss of life and high property damage. For more research, students can check the USGS website to find quakes that have happened on a certain day or within a radius of their location. One of the challenges of logarithmic scales is retaining the intuitive interpretation of a step. Allow students to practice this transition with the data included as well as data from other quakes that they can find online. They can continue the process of this task on their own data.
Supplies	Handouts
Mathematical Discourse	1. What types of events or phenomena have a range that is extremely large? Consider things as close and personal as the human body and as far away as space. How could you compare these on a single scale?
Writing/Discussion Prompts	1. Compare scientific notation to using a log scale. How are these representations similar? How are they different? 2. Consider the earthquake data included in this task. What surprises you about it? Why? Why do we not hear about smaller earthquakes? 3. Why doesn't twice the measurement on the Richter scale mean twice the intensity of the earthquake?

Curriculum Content	
CCSSM Content Standards	HSF-LE.1c, HSF-LE.5
CCSSM Mathematical Practices	2. Reason abstractly and quantitatively: Students must approach the meaning of a number line or a scale in a different context. 8. Students look for and express regularity in repeated reasoning: Students incorporate powers of 10 in their analysis of the magnitudes of different earthquakes.

Performance Task (continued)

Rubric

Measuring Natural Disasters	Points
1. Students can interpret and plot data. **Earthquakes by Magnitude** (graph with points: (5, 0.9), (1, 0.8), (5, 0.8), (2, 0.7), (4, 0.6), (6, 0.6), (3, 0.4), (2, 0.4), (9, 0.2), (4, 0.1), (8, 0.2), (3, 0), (7, 0), (5, −0.2), (1, −0.3), (7, −0.3))	**3** Graph is correct and labeled **2** Graph is mostly correct, or graph is correct but not labeled **1** Some of the graph is correct.
Students can interpret a logarithmic scale. *Sample answers:* 2. West Plains, MO 3. Prince William Sound, AK 4. San Francisco, CA 5. Tustin, CA; Prince William Sound, AK; Tustin, CA, at 1.3 to Prince William Sound, AK, at 9.2, 100 million times stronger $\left(\text{or } 10^8\right)$ 6. 10,000 times; The difference in magnitude is about 4 7. Prince William Sound and the San Francisco quakes; The difference in magnitude is about 1. 8. Fort Payne, AL, and Fukuoka, Japan, quakes; The difference in magnitude is about 2 . 9. Ocotillo Wells, CA, and Port-au-Prince, Haiti, quakes; The difference in magnitude is about 3. 10. Morristown, NJ, and Port-au-Prince, Haiti, quakes; The difference in magnitude is about 4. 11. Tustin, CA, and Fukushima, Japan, quakes; The difference in magnitude is about 6.	**10** All correct **7** Most correct **4** Some correct **2** Few correct You may also assign 1 point per correct answer.
Mathematics Practice: Students look for and express regularity in repeated reasoning. Students should be able to explain differences in magnitudes using both the scale and powers of 10.	**2** For demonstration of practice; Partial credit can be awarded.
Total Points	**15 points**

Chapter 6

Performance Task (continued)

Measuring Natural Disasters

In 2005, an earthquake measuring 4.1 on the Richter scale barely shook the city of Ocotillo, California, leaving virtually no damage. But in 1906, an earthquake with an estimated 8.2 on the same scale devastated the city of San Francisco. Does twice the measurement on the Richter scale mean twice the intensity of the earthquake?

In 1935, Charles Richter developed a method to compare the strength of earthquakes. Seismographs could already detect and record seismic waves. Richter's scale was a way to make sense of these measurements. A major challenge of such a scale was how to represent signals with such an enormous difference in intensity—the largest signals could be over one billion times greater than the smallest ones. The solution was to use a logarithmic scale. In a linear scale, units along the x-axis increase by a constant, usually 1. But in a log scale, units along the x-axis increase by powers of 10. An increase of 1 point means the strength of the earthquake is 10^1 times greater than the level before. An increase of 2 points means the strength of the earthquake is 10^2, or 100 times greater.

Earthquakes In Chronological Order[1]

Date	Location	Magnitude
April 18, 1906	San Francisco, California	8.2
March 28, 1964	Prince William Sound, Alaska	9.2
September 7, 1999	Athens, Greece	5.9
April 29, 2003	Fort Payne, Alabama	4.6
March 30, 2005	Fukuoka, Japan	6.6
May 20, 2005	Ocotillo Wells, California	4.1
December 16, 2005	Hercules, California	3.4
February 3, 2009	Morristown, New Jersey	3.0
January 12, 2010	Port-au-Prince, Haiti	7.0
August 23, 2011	Mineral, Virginia	5.8
August 29, 2011	West Plains, Missouri	2.4
October 16, 2012	Midlothian, Texas	2.7
June 11, 2013	Conway, Arkansas	1.8
October 25, 2013	Fukushima, Japan	7.3
December 24, 2013	Tustin, California	1.3
January 17, 2014	Jacó, Costa Rica	5.2

Chapter 6 **Performance Task** (continued)

1. Using the chart, plot and label the earthquake data according to magnitude. The *x*-axis represents the whole-number portion of the magnitude and the *y*-axis represents the decimal portion of the magnitude. For example, a quake of magnitude 5.3 occurring in Trinidad, Colorado, would be plotted and labeled as (5, 0.3) because its whole number is 5 and its decimal is 0.3.

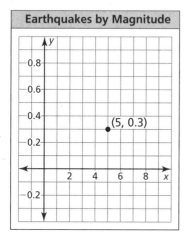

Earthquakes by Magnitude

2. What earthquake was about 10 times stronger than the quake in Tustin, California?

3. What earthquake was about 100 times stronger than the quake in Fukushima, Japan?

4. What earthquake was about 1000 times stronger than the quake in Jacó, Costa Rica?

5. What is the smallest earthquake in the data? What is the largest? Compare their magnitudes.

6. How much larger was the devastating San Francisco quake than the quake that barely shook Ocotillo Wells, California? Explain.

7. Find two earthquakes, other than the ones in Exercise 2, in which one was about 10 times stronger than the other. Explain how you chose these quakes.

8. Find two earthquakes, other than the ones in Exercise 3, in which one was about 100 times stronger than the other. Explain how you chose these quakes.

9. Find two earthquakes, other than the ones in Exercise 4, in which one was about 1000 times stronger than the other. Explain how you chose these quakes.

10. Find two earthquakes in which one was 10,000 times stronger than the other. Explain how you chose these quakes.

11. Find two earthquakes in which one was a million times stronger than the other. Explain how you chose these quakes.

Name_____ Date_____

Teacher Notes:

Chapters 4-6 **Quarterly Standards Based Test**

1. The synthetic division below represent $f(x) \div (x - 2)$. Choose a value for p so that $x - 2$ is a factor of f. Justify your answer. *(HSA-APR.B.2)*

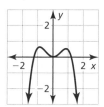

-1	-3	-5
1	3	5

2. Analyze the graph of the polynomial function to determine and explain the sign of the leading coefficient, the degree of the function, and the number of real zeros. *(HSF-IF.B.4)*

3. Which statement about the graph of $4(y + 5) = (x - 3)^2$ is *not* true? *(HSG-GPE.A.2)*

   A. The vertex is $(3, -5)$.

   B. The axis of symmetry is $x = 3$.

   C. The focus is $(3, 6)$.

   D. The graph represents a function.

4. Classify each function as *even*, *odd*, or *neither*. Justify your answer. *(HSF-BF.B.3)*

   a. $f(x) = -2x^5$ **b.** $f(x) = 5x^3 + 7x - 2$

   c. $f(x) = x^8 + x^6$ **d.** $f(x) = 4x^5 - 2x^3$

   e. $f(x) = 3x^6 + 4x^4 - 7x^2 + 6$ **f.** $f(x) = 5x^6 + 2x^3$

Chapters 4–6 Quarterly Standards Based Test (continued)

5. Select values for the function to model each transformation of the graph of $f(x) = x^2$.
   (HSF-BF.B.3)

   $$g(x) = \square(x - \square)^2 + \square$$

   a. The graph is a translation 4 units up and 3 units right.

   b. The graph is a translation 4 units left and 3 units down.

   c. The graph is a vertical shrink by a factor of $\frac{1}{3}$, followed by a translation
      4 units down.

   d. The graph is a translation 2 units left and a vertical stretch by a factor of 3, followed
      by a translation 3 units up.

6. The diagram shows a square inscribed in a circle. The area of the shaded region is
   32.1 square feet. To the nearest tenth of a foot, what is the radius of the circle?
   (HSA-REI.B.4b)

   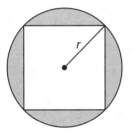

   A. 3.2 ft   **B.** 5.3 ft   **C.** 7.4 ft   **D.** 8.9 ft

7. The volume of the triangular prism shown is given by $V = x^3 - 7x - 6$. Which
   polynomial represents the area of the base of the prism? *(HSA-APR.B.2)*

   A. $x^2 + 2x - 3$

   B. $x^2 + 3 - 2x$

   C. $x^2 + 3 + 2x$

   D. $x^2 - 2x - 3$

   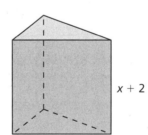

   $x + 2$

Chapters 4–6 **Quarterly Standards Based Test** (continued)

8. Identify and describe three pairs of equivalent expressions. Assume all variables are positive. *(HSA-RN.A.2)*

| $\sqrt[3]{b}$ | $\sqrt[3]{b^3}$ | $\sqrt[3]{b^2}$ | $b^{4/6}$ |

| b^3 | $b^{-2/3}$ | $b^{1/3}$ | b |

9. The graph represents the function $f(x) = \left| x - \square \right| + \square$. Choose the correct values to complete the function. *(HSF-BF.B.3)*

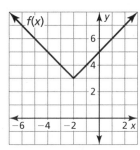

| -4 | -3 | -2 | -1 |

| 1 | 2 | 3 | 4 |

10. A polynomial function fits the data in the table. Use finite differences to find the degree of the function and complete the table. Explain your reasoning. *(HSF-BF.A.1a)*

x	-2	-1	0	1	2	3	4	5
$f(x)$	-47	-17	-9	-11	-11	3		

11. The area of the rectangle is 85 square centimeters. Find the value of x. *(HSA-REI.B.4b)*

x cm

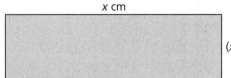

$(x - 12)$ cm

Chapters 4–6 **Quarterly Standards Based Test** (continued)

12. Which equations are functions? Which equations have an inverse function?
    Place check marks in the appropriate spaces. Explain your reasoning.
    (HSA-CED.A.2)

Equation	Function	Has Inverse Function
$y = \lvert x + 6 \rvert$		
$x = (y - 1)^2$		
$y = x^2 - 7$		
$x^2 = 4 - y^2$		

13. What is the solution of the inequality $8 - 3\sqrt{x - 1} > 2$? *(HSA-REI.A.2)*

    A. $x \geq 1$ **B.** $x < 5$

    C. $1 < x < 5$ **D.** $1 \leq x < 5$

14. Which function does the graph represent? Explain your reasoning. *(HSF-BF.B.3)*

    A. $y = -2(x - 1)^2$

    B. $y = -2x^2 + 1$

    C. $y = 2(x - 1)^2$

    D. $y = 2x^2 + 1$

    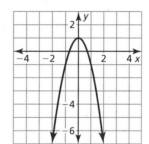

15. The graphs of two functions f and g are shown.
    Are f and g inverse functions? Explain your reasoning.
    (HSF-BF.B.4c)

    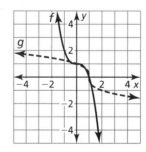

16. Select every value of b for the equation $y = \log_b x$ that could result in the graph shown. *(HSF-IF.C.8b)*

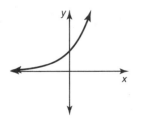

17. Your friend claims more interest is earned when an account pays a higher interest rate than when an account pays compound interest more times per year. Is your friend correct? Explain your reasoning. *(HSF-IF.B.4)*

18. You are designing a hollow foam ball. The ball has a thickness of 1 centimeter. *(HSF-BF.A.1a)*

   a. Let r represent the outside radius of the ball. Write a polynomial function $V(r)$ that gives the volume of the sphere formed by the outer surface of the ball.

   b. Write a polynomial function $W(r)$ for the volume of the inside of the ball.

   c. Let $S(r)$ be a polynomial function that represents the volume of the foam. How is $S(r)$ related to $V(r)$ and $W(r)$?

   d. Write $S(r)$ in standard form. What is the volume of the foam to the nearest tenth of a cubic centimeter when the radius of the ball is 12 centimeters?

19. What is the solution of the logarithmic inequality $-6 \log_4 x \geq -3$? *(HSA-CED.A.3)*

   A. $0 < x \leq 2$

   B. $0 \leq x \leq 2$

   C. $x \leq 2$

   D. $0 < x$

Chapters 4–6 **Quarterly Standards Based Test** (continued)

20. Describe the transformation of $f(x) = \log_3 x$ represented by the graph of g. *(HSF-BF.B.3)*

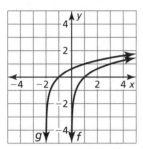

21. Let $f(x) = (2x + 3)^2$, $g(x) = 7x - 4x^2 + 2$, and $h(x) = 8x^3 - 9x + 3$. Order the following functions in order from least degree to greatest degree. *(HSA-SSE.A.1a)*

   A. $(f + g)(x)$ **B.** $(gh)(x)$

   C. $(g - h)(x)$ **D.** $(fg)(x)$

22. Choose a method to solve each quadratic equation. Explain your choice of method. *(HSA-REI.B.4b)*

   a. $(x - 2)^2 = 25$ **b.** $x^2 - 6x = -7$

   c. $x^2 + x - 20 = 0$ **d.** $4x - 3 = 2(x + 1)^2$

23. The winter months are the busiest tourist months in a Florida city. The table shows the average number y of rooms rented during a given year, where t is the month of the year ($t = 1$ corresponds to January). Create a scatter plot of the data. Does the data show a *linear*, *quadratic*, or *exponential* relationship? Use technology to find a model for the data. One specific month, the average number of rooms rented was 192. What month could it have been? *(HSF-LE.A.2)*

Month, t	1	2	3	4	5	6	7	8	9	10	11	12
Rooms, y	220	205	180	170	115	90	75	60	85	125	180	205

Chapter 7 Quiz

For use after Section 7.2

Tell whether *x* and *y* show *direct variation*, *inverse variation*, or *neither*.
Explain your reasoning.

Answers

1. $y = x - 2$ **2.** $\frac{3}{4}x = y$ **3.** $xy = 0.3$

4.

x	5	8	11	14
y	7	14	21	28

5.

x	8	4	2	1
y	32	16	8	4

6. The variables *x* and *y* vary inversely, and $y = 8$ when $x = 2$. Write an equation that relates *x* and *y*. Then find *y* when $x = -4$.

Match the equation with the correct graph.

7. $f(x) = \frac{5}{x} + 4$ **8.** $y = \frac{-3}{x + 1} - 2$ **9.** $h(x) = \frac{2x - 3}{4x + 2}$

A.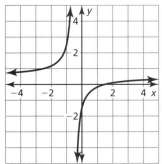

B.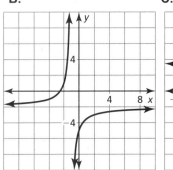

C.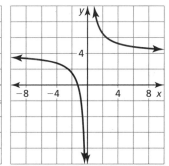

1. _____

   _____

2. _____

   _____

3. _____

   _____

4. _____

   _____

5. _____

   _____

6. _____

   _____

7. _____

8. _____

9. _____

10. _____

    _____

11. **See left.**

10. Rewrite $g(x) = \frac{2x + 12}{x + 3}$ in the form of $g(x) = \frac{a}{x - h} + k$. Describe the graph of *g* as a transformation of the graph of $f(x) = \frac{a}{x}$.

11. The time (in minutes) it takes for a leaky barrel to empty varies inversely with the rate at which the liquid is leaking (in gallons per minute). The leaking rate of a certain liquid is 3 gallons per minute, and it takes a barrel full of the liquid 30 minutes to empty. Complete the table for the times it takes to empty the barrel for the given rates.

Leaking rate (gal/min)	Time (min)
6	
8	
18	
24	
30	

Name_____ Date_____

The variables *x* and *y* vary inversely. Use the given values to write an equation relating *x* and *y*. Then find *y* when *x* = −2.

1. $x = 7, \ y = 2$

2. $x = 9, \ y = -\dfrac{13}{3}$

3. $x = -6, \ y = 5$

4. $x = \dfrac{8}{5}, \ y = \dfrac{5}{2}$

The graph shows the function $y = \dfrac{1}{x-h} + k$**. Determine whether the value of each constant *h* and *k* is *positive*, *negative*, or *zero*.**

5.
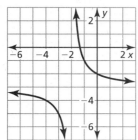

6.
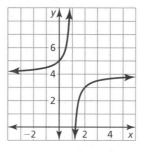

7.
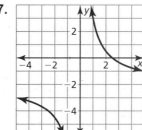

8.
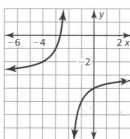

Perform the indicated operation.

9. $\dfrac{3x^3}{6y^2} \bullet \dfrac{4y^5}{7x^4}$

10. $\dfrac{x^2}{x-2} \bullet \dfrac{x^2 + 3x - 10}{x^2 + 2x}$

11. $\dfrac{x^2 + x - 6}{x^2 + 9x + 14} - \dfrac{8}{x+7}$

12. $\dfrac{x^2 + 3x + 2}{x^2 - 1} \bullet \dfrac{x^2 - 6x + 5}{x^2 + 5x + 6}$

13. $\dfrac{3h^3}{7j^5} \div \dfrac{18h}{21j^3}$

14. $\dfrac{1}{x+2} \bullet \dfrac{3}{x^2 - 4}$

15. A specialty muffin company makes muffins for $0.12 per muffin. The starting cost of the company is $300. How many muffins must the company make before the average cost per muffin is $0.25? Round your answer to the nearest whole number.

Answers

1. _____

_____

2. _____

_____

3. _____

_____

4. _____

_____

5. _____

_____

6. _____

_____

7. _____

_____

8. _____

_____

9. _____

10. _____

11. _____

12. _____

13. _____

14. _____

15. _____

Chapter 7 Test A (continued)

16. Your family plans to take a vacation this summer. For the cost of the vacation to be manageable, you determine that it will be in the best interest of your family to share a vacation home with other families. The cost c (in dollars) per family of the vacation home is inversely proportional to the number t of families sharing the house. Your family wants the cost of the house per family to be $600. Currently, with three families (including your family), the vacation home rental cost is $1000 per family. How many more families have to join to get the vacation home to be manageable for your family?

17. Simplify the equation $y = \dfrac{(x - 8)(x + 2)}{x + 2}$. Determine whether the graph of $f(x) = x - 8$ and the graph of $g(x) = y$ are different. Explain your reasoning below.

18. Five table tennis balls fit tightly in a rectangular box as shown below.

    a. Write an expression for the volume V of the rectangular box in terms of the radius r. Then rewrite the formula to express the radius in terms of the volume.

    b. Find the percent of the box's volume that is occupied by the table tennis balls. Use 3.14 for π.

19. A cab driver drove from the airport to a passenger's home at an average speed of 60 miles per hour. After the pickup, the cab driver returned with the passenger along the same route to the airport at an average speed of 50 miles per hour. What was the driver's average speed throughout the entire trip? Round your answer to the nearest hundredth.

Answers

16. _____

17. __See left.__

18. a._____

     _____

    b._____

19. _____

Chapter 7 Test B

The variables *x* and *y* vary inversely. Use the given values to write an equation relating *x* and *y*. Then find *y* when *x* = 2.

1. $x = -1, \ y = 29$

2. $x = 8, \ y = 11$

3. $x = 3, \ y = 12$

4. $x = \frac{3}{7}, \ y = \frac{7}{6}$

The graph shows the function $y = \dfrac{1}{x - h} + k$. Determine whether the value of each constant *h* and *k* is *positive*, *negative*, or *zero*.

5.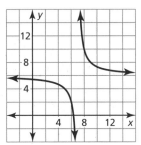

6.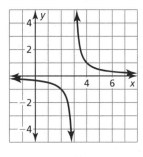

7.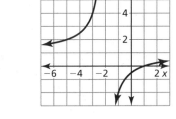

8.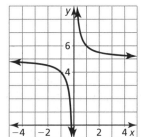

Perform the indicated operation.

9. $\dfrac{6a^2}{b} \div \dfrac{3a^4}{5b^2}$

10. $\dfrac{t^2 + 4t - 21}{t^2 + t - 12} - \dfrac{6}{t + 4}$

11. $\dfrac{x^2 - 2x - 35}{x^2 - 4x - 21} \div \dfrac{x^2 + 9x + 20}{x^2 - x - 12}$

12. $\dfrac{p^2}{p + 6} \cdot \dfrac{p^2 + 11p + 30}{p^2 + 6p}$

13. $\dfrac{7m^2}{3n^5} \cdot \dfrac{8n^6}{10m^4}$

14. $\dfrac{4}{m + 8} + \dfrac{1}{m^2 - 64}$

15. For Valentine's Day, a chocolate store plans to produce a chocolate-covered strawberry in the shape of a heart. The initial cost for the store to produce this item is $560. The store estimates that it will cost $0.84 to make one heart-shaped chocolate-covered strawberry. How many of the heart-shaped chocolate-covered strawberries must the company produce before the average cost for the item is $1.25? Round your answer to the nearest whole number.

Answers

1. _____

_____

2. _____

_____

3. _____

_____

4. _____

_____

5. _____

_____

6. _____

_____

7. _____

_____

8. _____

_____

9. _____

10. _____

11. _____

12. _____

13. _____

14. _____

15. _____

Chapter 7 **Test B** (continued)

16. The length s (in inches) of a cello string varies inversely as the frequency f of vibrations of the string. A cello string that is 6 inches long vibrates at a frequency of 600 cycles per second. Find the frequency at which a 9-inch cello string vibrates.

17. Simplify the equation $y = \dfrac{(x-3)(x-4)}{x-4}$. Determine whether the graph of $f(x) = x - 3$ and the graph of $g(x) = y$ are different. Explain your reasoning below.

Answers

16. _____

17. ___See left.___

18. a._____

_____

b._____

19. _____

18. Sixteen perfectly spherical tangerines fit tightly into the box shown below.

a. Write an expression for the volume V of the rectangular box in terms of the radius r. Then rewrite the formula to express the radius in terms of the volume.

b. Find the percent of the box's volume that is *not* occupied by the tangerines. Use 3.14 for π.

19. In chemistry class, you add a 70% iodide solution to 3 milliliters of a solution that is 15% iodide. The function $f(x) = \dfrac{3(0.15) + x(0.70)}{3 + x}$ represents the percent of iodide in the resulting solution, where x is the amount of 70% solution that is added. How much of the 70% iodide solution should be added to create a solution that is 40% iodide?

Name_____ Date_____

Alternative Assessment

1. Define a rational function $f(x)$

    a. that has zeros of -3 and 2 and no asymptotes. Graph the function.

    b. that has zeros of -3 and 2, one vertical asymptote at $x = 1$, and no horizontal asymptote. Graph the function.

    c. that has zeros of -3 and 2, one vertical asymptote at $x = 1$, and a horizontal asymptote at $y = 2$. Graph the function.

2. A standard beverage can has a volume of 21.7 cubic inches.

    a. Use the formula for the volume of a cylinder, $V = \pi r^2 h$, to write an equation that gives the height h of a standard beverage can in terms of its radius r.

    b. Using the expression for h from part (a) and the formula for the surface area of a cylinder, write an equation that gives the surface area of the beverage can S in terms of only its radius r. The formula for the surface area of a cylinder is $S = 2\pi r^2 + 2\pi rh$.

    c. Rewrite the equation for S from part (b) as a quotient of two polynomials. Will S have a horizontal asymptote? Explain.

    d. Use a graphing calculator to find the minimum value of S. What are the dimensions r and h of the can that use the least amount of material?

    e. Compare the dimensions r and h from part (d) with the dimensions of an actual beverage can, which has a radius of 1.25 inches and a height of 4.42 inches.

    f. Why might a manufacturer choose not to make the beverage can with the least amount of material possible?

Chapter 7 Alternative Assessment Rubric

Score	Conceptual Understanding	Mathematical Skills	Work Habits
4	Shows complete understanding of: • graphs of rational functions • operations on rational functions	All rational functions are defined and graphed correctly in Exercise 1. Equations for height and surface area are correct Correct minimum is found for equations given and explained	Answers all parts of all problems Answers are explained thoroughly with mathematical terminology. Work is very neat and well organized.
3	Shows nearly complete understanding of: • graphs of rational functions • operations on rational functions	All rational functions are defined correctly but not graphed correctly in Exercise 1. Either equation for height or surface area is incorrect Correct minimum is found for equations given and explained	Answers most parts of all problems Answers are explained with mathematical terminology. Work is neat and organized.
2	Shows some understanding of: • graphs of rational functions • operations on rational functions	At least one rational function is defined incorrectly in Exercise 1. Neither equation for height or surface area is correct Incorrect minimum is found for equations given	Answers some parts of all problems Answers are poorly or incorrectly explained. Work is not very neat or organized.
1	Shows little understanding of: • graphs of rational functions • operations on rational functions	At least two rational functions are defined incorrectly in Exercise 1. Neither equation for height or surface area is correct Incorrect minimum is found for equations given	Attempts few parts of any problem No explanation is included with answers. Work is sloppy and disorganized.

Name _____ Date _____

Circuit Design

Instructional Overview	
Launch Question	A thermistor is a resistor whose resistance varies with temperature. Thermistors are an engineer's dream because they are inexpensive, small, rugged, and accurate. The one problem with thermistors is their responses to temperature are not linear. How would you design a circuit that corrects this problem?
Summary	Students are given seven rational functions and must identify a pair that will sum to a linear function. Expressions have different denominators and degrees. There are two different pairs of thermistors that result in a linear sum and three distracter expressions.
Teacher Notes	Thermistors are a special kind of resistor used in all types of electronics. They are temperature sensors and found in many household appliances such as automatic ovens and air conditioning/heating system thermostats. There are two types of thermistors: PTC (Positive Temperature Coefficient) and NTC (Negative Temperature Coefficient). For a PTC thermistor, resistance increases as temperature increases. For a NTC thermistor, resistance decreases as temperature increases.
	Thermistors are not always easy to design. An engineer would like to detect temperature in a linear way, i.e. a constant change in temperature yields a constant change in resistance. This is not usually the case for a thermistor. They have very nonlinear characteristics. For this reason, circuit designers often use combinations of thermistors to obtain the type of temperature-sensing function they need.
	A good example of linear versus nonlinear behavior is a channel changer that either always changes the channel at the same rate or changes channels more quickly the longer the button is held down.
	Please note that the resistance functions defined in this task are not based on actual thermistor response curves but have been designed to make the algebraic calculations manageable. More information on thermistors can be found on the Internet.
Supplies	Handouts, graphing calculators
Mathematical Discourse	1. Explain what it means for a function to have a "linear response." How is this different from a "nonlinear response"?
	2. Why would a thermistor with a linear response be preferable?
Writing/Discussion Prompts	Create two rational functions such that their sum is a linear function.

Chapter 7 Performance Task (continued)

Circuit Design

Curriculum Content	
CCSSM Content Standards	HSA-SSE.3, HSA-APR.D.1, HSA-APR.D.6, HSA-APR.D.7
CCSSM Mathematical Practices	2. Make sense of problems and persevere in solving them. Students will have to sort through seven rational functions to identify a specific pair that meet the criteria. They will quickly see that this task will take a very long time unless they can eliminate choices strategically.
	4. Model with mathematics. The non-linearity of thermistors and circuit design is a real-life problem.
	5. Use appropriate tools strategically. Students can save time by using a graphing calculator and the table of values to graph combinations of thermistors. The graphing function also gives them a second way of verifying that their circuit does indeed behave linearly.

Rubric

Circuit Design	Points	
Students can use a graphing calculator to enter rational functions with correct syntax. Note that this skill can be observed on parts 1 and 3, or students can sketch each rational function on a separate sheet of paper.	**3**	Graphs are always correct.
	2	Graphs are usually correct.
	1	Graphs are rarely correct.
Students can add, subtract, and simplify rational functions. Pairs that simplify to linear functions are Thermistors 2 and 3, and Thermistors 5 and 7. Students provide explanation of how correct pairs were determined.	**5**	Both pairs are correct.
	3	One pair is correct.
	1	Neither pair is correct but some algebraic operations, such as factoring, were accurate.
Mathematics Practice: 2. Make sense of problems and persevere in solving them. Students explain their strategies for choosing thermistor pairs to test, either written or verbally.	**2**	For demonstration of practice. Partial credit can be awarded.
Total Points	**10 points**	

Name _____ Date _____

Circuit Design

A thermistor is a resistor whose resistance varies with temperature. Thermistors are an engineer's dream because they are inexpensive, small, rugged, and accurate. The one problem with thermistors is their responses to temperature are not linear. How would you design a circuit that corrects this problem?

A series circuit is a circuit in which resistors are arranged in a chain. The total resistance of the circuit is found by adding the resistance of each individual resistor in the chain. This type of design is sometimes used to make the total resistance of the circuit more linear with respect to a given variable or input. In the case of the thermistor, this variable is temperature.

A series circuit along with a set of thermistors and their outputs is shown below.

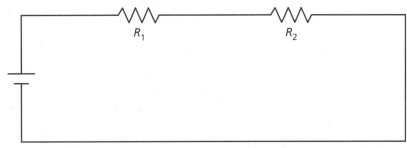

A series circuit: $R_{total}(t) = R_1(t) + R_2(t)$, where t is temperature

Therm$_1$:	Therm$_2$:	Therm$_3$:	Therm$_4$:
$R(t) = \dfrac{t-2}{t+2}$	$R(t) = \dfrac{t^2}{t-2}$	$R(t) = \dfrac{4}{2-t}$	$R(t) = \dfrac{4t}{t-2}$

Therm$_5$:	Therm$_6$:	Therm$_7$:
$R(t) = \dfrac{t^3}{t^2+2t+4}$	$R(t) = \dfrac{(t+2)^2}{t^2+2t+4}$	$R(t) = \dfrac{-8}{t^2+2t+4}$

1. With a graphing calculator, verify that the resistance of each individual thermistor is nonlinear.

2. Using what you have learned about operations on rational functions, how would you design this circuit so that the total resistance, $R_1 + R_2$, is linear? Which pairs of thermistors will work?

3. Verify algebraically and graphically that your final circuit has a linear total resistance.

4. Explain the process that you used to choose and test your thermistors. Was your approach random? Did you test every pair? What characteristics about each rational function were important?

Name _____ Date _____

Chapter 8 Quiz
For use after Section 8.3

Find the next term in the pattern and then write a rule for the *n*th term.

1. 2, 9, 16, 23, …   **2.** −3, 6, −9, 12, …   **3.** $\frac{1}{5}, \frac{2}{10}, \frac{3}{15}, \frac{4}{20}, \dots$

Write the series using summation notation. Then find the sum of the series.

4. $1 + 2 + 3 + \dots + 12$ **5.** $\frac{1}{2} + \frac{1}{4} + \frac{1}{6} + \dots + \frac{1}{14}$

Write a rule for the *n*th term of the sequence.

6.
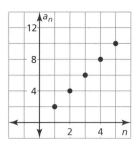

7.
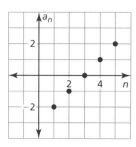

Tell whether the sequence is *arithmetic*, *geometric*, or *neither*. Write a rule for the *n*th term of the sequence. Then find a_9.

8. −20, −16, −12, −8, …

9. $\frac{2}{3}, \frac{3}{4}, \frac{4}{5}, \dots$

10. −1, 4, −16, 64, …

11. One term of an arithmetic sequence is $a_9 = 25$. The common difference is $d = 4$. Write a rule for the *n*th term.

Find the sum.

12. $\displaystyle\sum_{n=1}^{7}(2n - 3)$ **13.** $\displaystyle\sum_{k=1}^{6}9(-2)^{k-1}$

14. You are buying a new snowmobile. You take out a five-year loan for $8000. The annual interest rate of the loan is 5.4%. Use the monthly payment formula $M = \dfrac{L}{\displaystyle\sum_{k=1}^{t}\left(\dfrac{1}{1 + i}\right)^{k}}$ to calculate the monthly payment.

a. What will the monthly payment be for the snowmobile?

b. How much less will your monthly payment be if you take out a six-year loan at 5.8%?

Answers

1. _____

_____

2. _____

_____

3. _____

_____

4. _____

_____

5. _____

_____

6. _____

7. _____

8. _____

_____

_____

9. _____

_____

_____

10. _____

_____

_____

11. _____

12. _____

13. _____

14. a._____

b._____

Name_____ Date _____

Find the sum.

Answers

1. $\displaystyle\sum_{i=3}^{6}(2i - 2)$

2. $\displaystyle\sum_{i=1}^{5}3 \bullet 4^i$

3. $\displaystyle\sum_{k=1}^{4}(-1)^k(k + 18)$

4. $\displaystyle\sum_{n=1}^{5}11$

5. $\displaystyle\sum_{i=1}^{50}(5i - 4)$

6. $\displaystyle\sum_{i=1}^{\infty}5(-0.3)^{i-1}$

1. _____

2. _____

3. _____

4. _____

5. _____

Determine whether the graph represents an arithmetic sequence, geometric sequence, or neither. Then write a rule for the *n*th term.

6. _____

7. _____

7.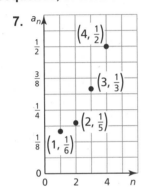

8.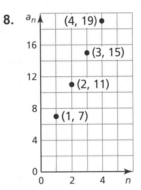

_____

8. _____

_____

9. _____

9.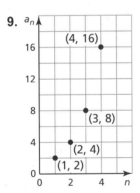

10.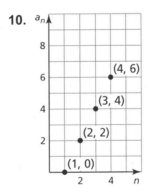

_____

10. _____

_____

11. _____

_____

12. _____

Write a recursive rule for the sequence. Then find a_7.

11. $-3, 6, -12, 24, \ldots$

12. $a_n = 4n + 4$

_____

13. _____

13. $a_1 = 16; r = \dfrac{1}{4}$

14. $-2, -5, -8, -11, \ldots$

_____

14. _____

15. Write a recursive rule for the sequence $5, 2, -1, -4, \ldots$. Then write an explicit rule for the sequence using the recursive rule.

_____

15. _____

_____

Chapter 8 Test A (continued)

16. Use the diagram of the stacking of cans below to answer the following questions.

   a. What does *n* represent? What does a_n represent?

   b. Complete the table that shows *n* and a_n for *n* = 1, 2, 3, 4, 5, 6, 7, 8.

n	a_n
1	
2	
3	
4	
5	
6	
7	
8	

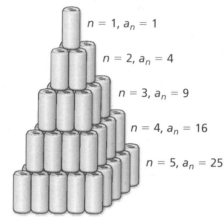

$n = 1, a_n = 1$
$n = 2, a_n = 4$
$n = 3, a_n = 9$
$n = 4, a_n = 16$
$n = 5, a_n = 25$

   c. Write an explicit rule that represents this situation.

17. As part of a retirement savings plan, you recently deposited $150 in a bank account during your first year in the workforce. During each subsequent year, you deposit $25 more than the previous year.

   a. How much money will you deposit in your 20th year in the workforce?

   b. Find the *total* amount of money you have deposited for all 20 years.

18. For art class, the teacher has asked you to create an image in which you draw equilateral triangles like those shown on the right. The first triangle has a perimeter of 20 inches. Each successive triangle has a perimeter that is 75% of the previously drawn triangle.

   a. What will the perimeter be of the fifth triangle? Round your answer to the nearest thousandth.

   b. If this process of drawing equilateral triangles continues until 6 triangles are drawn, what will be the total perimeter of all the triangles? Round your answer to the nearest thousandth.

Answers

16. a._____

_____

b.____See left.____

c._____

17. a._____

b._____

18. a._____

b._____

Name_____ Date_____

Chapter 8 Test B

Find the sum.

Answers

1. $\displaystyle\sum_{i=1}^{49}(4i - 3)$

2. $\displaystyle\sum_{i=3}^{6}5$

3. $\displaystyle\sum_{i=1}^{\infty}9(-0.2)^{i-1}$

1. _____

2. _____

4. $\displaystyle\sum_{i=1}^{5}\frac{4}{3}\cdot 4^{i}$

5. $\displaystyle\sum_{i=2}^{5}(4i - 5)$

6. $\displaystyle\sum_{i=1}^{4}(-1)^{t}(t + 5)$

3. _____

4. _____

Determine whether the graph represents an arithmetic sequence, geometric sequence, or neither. Then write a rule for the *n*th term.

5. _____

7.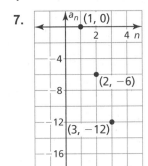

8.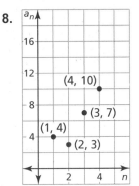

6. _____

7. _____

_____

8. _____

_____

9. _____

9.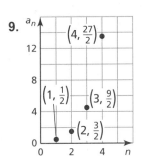

10.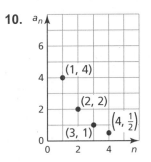

_____

10. _____

_____

11. _____

Write a recursive rule for the sequence. Then find a_6.

_____

11. $-2, -7, -12, -17, \dots$

12. $r = \frac{1}{5}, a_1 = 125$

12. _____

_____

13. $a_n = 3 - 2n$

14. $2, 9, 37, 149, \dots$

13. _____

_____

15. Write a recursive rule for the sequence $-3, 9, -27, 81, \dots$. Then write an explicit rule for the sequence using the recursive rule.

14. _____

_____

15. _____

_____

16. Use the diagram of the stacking of oranges below to answer the following questions.

a. What does n represent? What does a_n represent?

b. Complete the table that shows n and a_n for $n = 1, 2, 3, 4, 5, 6, 7, 8$.

n	a_n
1	
2	
3	
4	
5	
6	
7	
8	

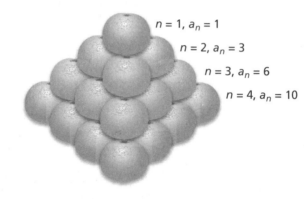

$n = 1, a_n = 1$

$n = 2, a_n = 3$

$n = 3, a_n = 6$

$n = 4, a_n = 10$

Answers

16. a._____

   _____

b.___See left.___

c._____

17. a._____

b._____

18. _____

19. a._____

b._____

c. Write an explicit rule that represents this situation.

17. You recently have been offered a job that pays you a monthly salary of $3500 and guarantees you a monthly raise of $180 during your first year on the job.

a. Find the general term of this arithmetic sequence.

b. What will your monthly salary be at the end of your first year of work?

18. In preparation to buy a new video game that costs $65, your friend plans on saving money each month for the purchase of the game. Your friend initially starts her savings with $10 in January, and plans on saving 10% more during each successive month. After what month will your friend be able to purchase the video game?

19. A math drawing asks that you create a design in which you draw squares within squares like the figure shown to the right. The first square has a perimeter of 8 inches. Each successive square has a perimeter that is 80% of the square immediately outside of it.

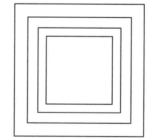

a. What will be the perimeter of the fourth square?

b. If this process of drawing the squares continues until seven squares are drawn, what will be the total perimeter of all the squares? Round your answer to the nearest thousandth.

Chapter 8 **Alternative Assessment**

1. To raise money for a local charity, the athletic boosters at your school are sponsoring a Half-Court Shootout during basketball season. During halftime, students can purchase the chance to make a half-court shot and win a cash prize. The prize increases by $50 with each game for which there is no winner. On the sixth game, you are the first winner, taking home $350.

   a. Classify the sequence of prize money per game as arithmetic, geometric, or neither. Explain.

   b. How much was the initial prize offered for the first game?

   c. Write a rule to determine the prize money for any game, assuming there were no winners in previous games.

   d. How large would the jackpot have been at the end of the team's 25-game season assuming there were no winners before the last game?

2. You and your parents are working on a scrapbook representing your family tree. You would like to include one page for the biography of each ancestor, and your parents want you to include a page on yourself.

   a. Classify the number of ancestors in each generation as an arithmetic sequence, a geometric sequence, or neither. Explain.

   b. Write a rule to model the number of people in each generation with the first generation including only yourself, the second your two parents, the third your four grandparents, and so on.

   c. How many generations can you include in the book if you must keep it to fewer than 300 pages?

   d. Assuming that one generation spans about 30 years, what year will your book begin?

   e. How many pages would you need for 12 generations of ancestors?

Chapter 8 Alternative Assessment Rubric

Score	Conceptual Understanding	Mathematical Skills	Work Habits
4	Shows complete understanding of: • arithmetic sequences • geometric sequences and series	The correct sequence type and formula are identified for both Exercises 1 and 2. All secondary calculations, such as the nth term and sum, are correct.	Answers all parts of all problems Answers are explained thoroughly with mathematical terminology. Work is very neat and well organized.
3	Shows nearly complete understanding of: • arithmetic sequences • geometric sequences and series	The correct sequence type and formula are identified for both Exercises 1 and 2. No more than one secondary calculation, such as the nth term and sum, are incorrect for either Exercise 1 or 2.	Answers most parts of all problems Answers are explained with mathematical terminology. Work is neat and organized.
2	Shows some understanding of: • arithmetic sequences • geometric sequences and series	The correct sequence type and formula are incorrect for Exercises 1 or 2. Several secondary calculations, such as the nth term and sum, are incorrect for either Exercise 1 or 2.	Answers some parts of all problems Answers are poorly or incorrectly explained. Work is not very neat or organized.
1	Shows little understanding of: • arithmetic sequences • geometric sequences and series	The correct sequence type and formula are incorrect for Exercise 1 and 2. Most secondary calculations, such as the nth term and sum, are incorrect for either Exercise 1 or 2.	Attempts few parts of any problem No explanation is included with answers. Work is sloppy and disorganized.

Name_____ Date_____

Performance Task

Integrated Circuits and Moore's Law

Instructional Overview	
Launch Question	In April of 1965, an engineer named Gordon Moore noticed how quickly the size of electronics was shrinking. He predicted how the number of transistors that could fit on a 1-inch diameter circuit would increase over time. In 1965, 50 transistors could fit on the circuit. A decade later, about 65,000 transistors could fit on the circuit. Moore's prediction was accurate and is now known as Moore's Law. What was his prediction? How many transistors will be able to fit on a 1-inch circuit when you graduate from high school?
Summary	Students characterize and investigate the geometric sequence that is used to make key predictions in the world of computing.
Teacher Notes	Whenever we are in awe of how quickly our computers and cell phones become obsolete, we are seeing the effects of Moore's Law. Moore's Law is a rule of thumb rather than a physical law, and fundamentally says that the complexity of technology doubles every 2 years. The law began with the prediction of doubling every year.
	Students may struggle with the concept that Moore's Law gives approximate numbers rather than exact, precise answers.
	Moore's original paper, *"Cramming More Components Onto Integrated Circuits,"* can be found at: http://www.cs.utexas.edu/~fussell/courses/cs352h/papers/moore.pdf
	A subsequent article by Moore, *"Moore's Law at 40,"* includes student-friendly metaphors and examples to help visualize large orders of magnitude, including the number of ants and grains of rice in the world. That article can be found at: http://www.ece.ucsb.edu/~strukov/ece15bSpring2011/others/MooresLawat40.pdf
	More information on Moore and his law can be found at: http://www.computerhistory.org/semiconductor/timeline/1965-Moore.html
Supplies	Handouts, graphing calculators
Mathematical Discourse	What does it mean for a video to "go viral?" What other things in your environment can "go viral?"
Writing/Discussion Prompts	1. The price of a candy bar in 1965 was five cents. If the price had increased according to Moore's Law, how much would a candy bar cost today? Explain.
	2. What other phenomena behave according to Moore's Law?
	3. What limitations and circumstances might slow down Moore's Law?

Chapter 8 Performance Task (continued)

Integrated Circuits and Moore's Law

Curriculum Content	
CCSSM Content Standards	HSF-LE.1, HSF-LE.2, HSF-LE.3, HSA-SSE.3c
CCSSM Mathematical Practices	4. Model with mathematics. Students create the sequence determined by Moore's Law and define a rule for it. This law still guides the growth of the complexity of technology.

Rubric

Integrated Circuits and Moore's Law	Points	
Students can use and compare linear and exponential regression. 1. a. $f(t) = 6495t + 50$ b. $f(t) = 50(2.05)^t$ 2. The exponential model is correct. The linear model evaluated for $t = 5$ is $f(5) = 32{,}525$. The exponential gives $f(5) = 1810$.	**3** **2** **1**	All correct 2 correct 1 correct
Students understand geometric sequences. 3. 50, 102, 210, 430, 883, 1810, 3711, 7607, 15,595, 31,970, 65,540; geometric with a common ratio of 2.05 4. $a_n = 50(2.05)^{n-1}$ 5. The number of transistors on a chip will double about every year. 6. The exponent would change to $\dfrac{(n-1)}{2}$. 7. $f(t) = 65{,}540(2.05)^{(n-1)/2}$, where n is the number of years since 1975; Answers depend on the year and include 2015: about 7.8×10^{10}; 2017 : 1.6×10^{11}	**5** **3** **1**	All correct 3 correct 1 correct
Mathematics Practice: 4. Model with mathematics.	**2**	For demonstration of practice partial credit can be awarded.
Total Points	**10 points**	

Name _____ Date _____

 Chapter 8 **Performance Task** (continued)

Integrated Circuits and Moore's Law

In April of 1965, an engineer named Gordon Moore noticed how quickly the size of electronics was shrinking. He predicted how the number of transistors that could fit on a 1-inch diameter circuit would increase over time. In 1965, 50 transistors could fit on the circuit. A decade later, about 65,000 transistors could fit on the circuit. Moore's prediction was accurate and is now known as Moore's Law. What was his prediction? How many transistors will be able to fit on a 1-inch circuit when you graduate from high school?

1. Using the given information and the *regression* feature on your graphing calculator, create a linear and an exponential model for Moore's Law. Let 1965 represent the initial time, $t = 0$. Round to the nearest hundredth, if necessary.

   a. linear model

   b. exponential model

2. In 1970, about 1800 transistors could fit on the semiconductor. Given this information, which model for Moore's Law is correct? Explain.

3. Write a sequence of terms representing the number of transistors that could fit on a one-inch diameter circuit from 1965 to 1975. Is the sequence arithmetic or geometric? Why?

4. Write a rule for the *n*th term of the sequence.

5. This sequence is known as "Moore's Law." Summarize Moore's Law in your own words.

6. In the 1970s, Moore revised his prediction to say that the number of transistors would double every two years. How does this affect the rule for your sequence?

7. Write a rule for a sequence that represents the number of transistors that could fit on a 1-inch diameter circuit from 1975 on using Moore's revised prediction. Using that rule, predict how many transistors will be able to fit on a circuit in the year that you graduate.

Name _____ Date _____

1. In a right triangle, θ is an acute angle and $\sin \theta = \frac{4}{9}$. Evaluate the other five **Answers**
   trigonometric functions of θ.

   1. _____

Find the value of x for the right triangle.

2.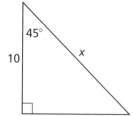

   45°
   10
   x

3.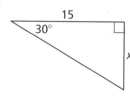

   15
   30°
   x

   _____

   _____

   _____

   _____

   2. _____

Find one positive angle and one negative angle that are coterminal with the
given angle.

   3. _____

   4. _____

4. 50°

5. $\frac{5\pi}{4}$

6. 800°

   5. _____

   6. _____

Convert the degree measure to radians or the radian measure to degrees.

   7. _____

7. $\frac{7\pi}{8}$

8. −80°

9. 64°

   8. _____

Evaluate the six trigonometric functions of θ.

   9. _____

10.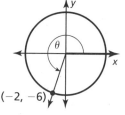

    θ
    x
    (−2, −6)

11.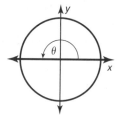

    θ
    x

    10. _____

    11. _____

12. Identify the amplitude and period of $g(x) = 5 \sin x$. Then describe the graph
    of g as a transformation of the graph of $f(x) = \sin x$.

    12. _____

13. You and some friends ride the carousel at an amusement park. The carousel
    has a radius of 25 feet and makes one revolution in 12 seconds. You sit on the
    very outside and ride for 5 minutes. Compare the distance you revolve with
    the distance of a friend who was seated 8 feet from the outside edge.

    13. _____

Name_____ Date_____

Verify the identity.

Answers

1. $\dfrac{(\sin x + \cos x)^2}{1 + 2 \sin x \cos x} = 1$

2. $\sin\left(x + \dfrac{\pi}{2}\right) = \cos x$

1. ___See left.___

2. ___See left.___

3. ___See left.___

4. _____

5. _____

6. _____

3. $\dfrac{\sin x - \cos x}{\sin x} + \dfrac{\cos x - \sin x}{\cos x} = 2 - \sec x \csc x$

7. _____

8. _____

9. _____

10. _____

Evaluate without using a calculator.

4. $\sec\left(-\dfrac{\pi}{3}\right)$

5. $\tan(405°)$

6. $\csc(-120°)$

Write a function for the sinusoid.

7.
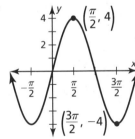

8.
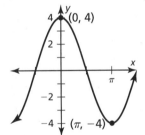

9.
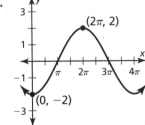

10.
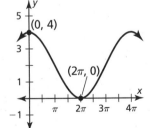

Chapter 9 Test A (continued)

Graph the function. Then describe the graph of _g_ as a transformation of the graph of its parent function.

11. $g(x) = 2 \tan 2x$

12. $g(x) = \sec 2x + 2$

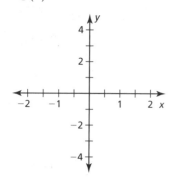

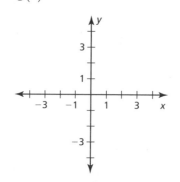

Convert the degree measure to radians or the radian measure to degrees. Then find one positive angle and one negative angle that is coterminal with the given angle.

13. $\dfrac{5\pi}{7}$

14. $-130°$

15. $\dfrac{13\pi}{4}$

16. Find the arc length and area of a sector with radius $r = 60$ inches and central angle $\theta = 30°$. Round your answer to the nearest hundredth.

Evaluate the given trigonometric function using the graph.

17. $\sec \theta$ **18.** $\csc \theta$

19. $\tan \theta$ **20.** $\cos \theta$

21. $\sin \theta$ **22.** $\cot \theta$

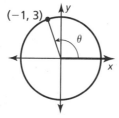

23. In what quadrant does the terminal side of θ lie when $\tan \theta < 0$ and $\sin \theta < 0$?

24. A radio transmission tower at your local television station is 130 feet tall, as shown in the figure. How long should a guy wire be if it is to be attached 14 feet below the top of the tower and make a $30°$ angle with the ground?

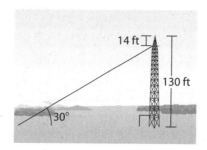

Answers

11. ___See left.___

_____

_____

12. ___See left.___

_____

_____

13. _____

_____

14. _____

_____

15. _____

_____

16. _____

17. _____

18. _____

19. _____

20. _____

21. _____

22. _____

23. _____

24. _____

Chapter 9 Test B

Verify the identity.

Answers

1. $\sin^2 x + \sin^2 x \cot^2 x = 1$

2. $1 - \dfrac{\cos^2 x}{1 + \sin x} = \sin x$

1. ____See left.____

2. ____See left.____

3. ____See left.____

4. _____

5. _____

6. _____

3. $\cos\left(x - \dfrac{5\pi}{6}\right) = -\dfrac{\sqrt{3}}{2} \cos x + \dfrac{1}{2} \sin x$

7. _____

8. _____

9. _____

10. _____

Evaluate without using a calculator.

4. $\csc\left(-\dfrac{\pi}{3}\right)$

5. $\cot(495°)$

6. $\sec(-240°)$

Write a function for the sinusoid.

7.
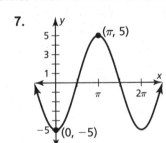

8.
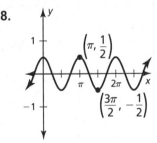

9.
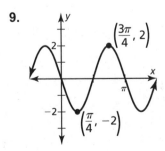

10.
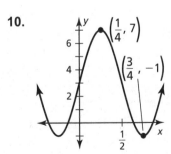

Chapter 9 **Test B** (continued)

Graph the function. Then describe the graph of *g* as a transformation of the graph of its parent function.

11. $g(x) = \frac{1}{3} \cot \frac{1}{2}x$

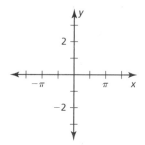

12. $g(x) = \csc(2\pi x)$

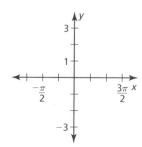

Answers

11. ___**See left.**___

_____

_____

12. ___**See left.**___

_____

_____

13. _____

_____

Convert the degree measure to radians or the radian measure to degrees. Then find one positive angle and one negative angle that is coterminal with the given angle.

14. _____

_____

13. $-560°$

14. $\frac{3\pi}{5}$

15. $170°$

15. _____

16. Find the arc length and area of a sector with radius $r = 10$ inches and central angle $\theta = 70°$. Round your answer to the nearest hundredth.

_____

16. _____

Evaluate the given trigonometric function using the graph.

17. _____

17. $\sec \theta$ **18.** $\csc \theta$

18. _____

19. $\tan \theta$ **20.** $\cos \theta$

21. $\sin \theta$ **22.** $\cot \theta$

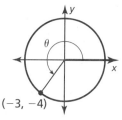

$(-3, -4)$

19. _____

20. _____

21. _____

23. In what quadrant does the terminal side of θ lie when $\cot \theta > 0$ and $\cos \theta < 0$?

22. _____

24. The table below shows the height h (in feet) as a function of the time t (in seconds) for a ride on the local Ferris wheel. Write a sine model that represents this situation.

23. _____

24. _____

Time (seconds)	0	1	2	3	4	5	6	7	8	9	10
Height (feet)	5	10	20	31	41	45	41	31	20	10	5

Chapter 9 Alternative Assessment

1. The terminal side of an angle θ is in Quadrant III and $\tan \theta = \dfrac{2\sqrt{5}}{5}$.

   Find each value.

   a. $\sin \theta$

   b. $\csc \theta$

   c. $\cos \theta$

   d. $\sec \theta$

   e. $\cot \theta$

2. The cap of the valve stem of a standard 26-inch bicycle tire is 11.5 inches from the center of the wheel. Suppose the wheel has an initial position such that the valve stem cap is closest to the ground as in the picture shown.

   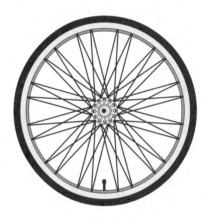

   a. Sketch a graph of the height of the valve stem cap as the bicycle travels forward along the road. Is this a periodic function? Explain.

   b. After the wheel has turned 90°, how high is the cap?

   c. After the wheel has turned 180°, how high is the cap?

   d. After the wheel has turned 510°, how high is the cap?

Name _____ Date _____

Score	Conceptual Understanding	Mathematical Skills	Work Habits
4	Shows complete understanding of: • right angle trigonometry • trigonometric functions • periodic functions	All answers in Exercise 1 and 2 are correct. The graph in Exercise 2 is continuous and clearly periodic in nature, repeating its maximum height at 24.5 inches. The minimum height may be labeled as 0 or 1.5 inches.	Answers all parts of all problems Answers are explained thoroughly with mathematical terminology. Work is very neat and well organized.
3	Shows nearly complete understanding of: • right angle trigonometry • trigonometric functions • periodic functions	One answer in Exercise 1 is incorrect, either in sign or value and/or one answer in Exercise 2 is incorrect. The graph in Exercise 2 is continuous and clearly periodic in nature, but a consistent maximum and minimum height are not clear.	Answers most parts of all problems Answers are explained with mathematical terminology. Work is neat and organized.
2	Shows some understanding of: • right angle trigonometry • trigonometric functions • periodic functions	Two or three answers in Exercise 1 are incorrect, either in sign or value and/or one answer in Exercise 2 is incorrect. The graph in Exercise 2 is somewhat periodic in nature but not necessarily continuous.	Answers some parts of all problems Answers are poorly or incorrectly explained. Work is not very neat or organized.
1	Shows little understanding of: • right angle trigonometry • trigonometric functions • periodic functions	Four or five answers in Exercise 1 are incorrect, either in sign or value and at least one answer in Exercise 2 is incorrect. The graph in Exercise 2 is clearly not periodic or is omitted.	Attempts few parts of any problem No explanation is included with answers. Work is sloppy and disorganized.

Name_____ Date_____

Performance Task

Lightening the Load

Instructional Overview	
Launch Question	You need to move a heavy table across the room. What is the easiest way to move it? Should you push it? Should you tie a rope around one leg of the table and pull it? How can trigonometry help you make the right decision?
Summary	Students learn how to calculate work and use the behavior of the cosine function to explain why it is best to apply force parallel to the direction of motion when moving an object.
Teacher Notes	Students may be new to the SI units of force (Newtons) and work (Joules). A good comparison of one Newton of force is about the force that it takes to keep a medium-sized apple or a stick of margarine from falling.
	Students will first calculate work directly in this activity, but then they will solve for a different variable, the force, when investigating the effects of cosine in the equation. The key is cosine decreases as the angle increases, so for work to remain constant, another factor in the equation must increase (either the force or the distance). If distance stays the same, the factor that increases must be the force.
	They will use the concept of parallel and perpendicular forces for the last question and may need reminders of these definitions from geometry.
Supplies	Handouts, graphing calculators
Mathematical Discourse	How does mathematics help you make decisions in your everyday life? Can math actually make your life easier?
Writing/Discussion Prompts	How would the relationship between work and the angle between the force and direction of motion change if work were defined in terms of sine?

Curriculum Content	
CCSSM Content Standards	HSF-TF.7, HSA-CED.4
CCSSM Mathematical Practices	3. Construct viable arguments and critique the reasoning of others. Some aspects of work are not intuitive, such as the fact that there must be displacement before work exists. Students will have to rely on the equation for work to explain this. 4. Model with mathematics. Students are familiar with the idea of work and incorporate trigonometry to explain their intuition.

Chapter 9 **Performance Task** (continued)

Rubric

Lightening the Load	Points
Students can evaluate the cosine function. 1. about 52 Joules 2. $W = 0$ Joule; Because no displacement took place, no work was done.	**2** Both answers are correct. **1** One answer is correct.
Students understand the behavior of the cosine function. 3. a. $W = 700$ Joules b. 355.4 Newtons c. 495 Newtons d. *Sample answer:* As the angle between the force and the direction of motion increases, the force required to do the same amount of work also increases. This is because the cosine $= 1$, its largest, for the angle of $0°$. This means the force and motion are going in the exact same direction. Cosine decreases as the angle increases. So, to hold the work constant, the force must increase. e. parallel to the force in the same direction f. The force should be almost perpendicular to the motion because $\cos(90°) = 0$.	**10** All answers are correct and explanations are thorough. **7** Answers are correct but explanations are missing or not thorough. **5** Some answers are incorrect. **2** Many answers are incorrect.
Mathematics Practice: 3. Construct viable arguments and critique the reasoning of others. Students should include logical and thorough reasoning.	**3** For demonstration of practice. Partial credit can be awarded.
Total Points	**15 points**

Name_____ Date _____

Lightening the Load

You need to move a heavy table across the room. What is the easiest way to move it? Should you push it? Should you tie a rope around one leg of the table and pull it? How can trigonometry help you make the right decision?

In general, we think of work as anything that requires effort, like homework, or going to work , meaning a job, or doing work around the house, meaning chores. But in math and physics, the idea of work is very specific and relies on trigonometry. This definition of work requires a force to act upon an object and for that object to move due to the applied force. The amount of work done depends on the strength of the force F, the distance d that the object moves, and the angle θ between the force and the direction of the motion. Work is measured in a unit called Joules and is defined by

$W = F \bullet d \bullet \cos \theta.$

1. Find the work required to pull a wheeled backpack at a $30°$ angle for 15 meters using a force of 4 Newtons.

2. How much work are you doing when you push against a wall using a force of 2000 Newtons? Explain your answer.

3. How does the angle of the force applied to the object affect the force required to move it?

   a. Suppose you are pushing a table with a horizontal force of 350 Newtons. If you move the table 2 meters, how much work have you done?

   b. Now suppose that instead of pushing the table for 2 meters, you drag it with a rope. You've tied the rope to a table leg and pull it such that the rope is at a $10°$ angle with the floor. How much force must you use to do the same amount of work as in part (a)?

   c. How much force must you use to do the same amount of work if you tie the rope to the table leg at a $45°$ angle?

   d. Compare your answers in parts (a), (b), and (c). Then use trigonometry to explain how the angle of the force applied to an object affects the force required to move it.

   e. In what direction should you apply force to an object if you want to minimize the force required to move it?

   f. Describe the physical circumstances requiring the greatest amount of force to move an object. Use mathematics to explain why this is true.

Name _____ Date _____

1. Which of the following functions are shown in the graph? Justify your answers.
   (HSF-IF.B.4)

   A. $y = -(x - 2)(x - 6)$

   B. $y = -3(x - 4)^2 + 12$

   C. $y = x^2 - 8x + 12$

   D. $y = -3x^2 + 24x - 36$

   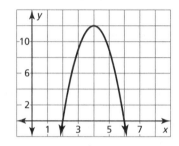

2. The graph of a rational function has asymptotes that intersect at the point $(2, 3)$. Choose the correct values to complete the equation of the function. Then graph the function.
   (HSF-IF.C.7d)

   $$y = \dfrac{\square x + 9}{\square x + \square}$$

12	−4
8	−8
4	−12

3. The tables below give the balances A (in dollars) owed on two different loans over time t (in years). *(HSS-ID.B.6a)*

Loan #1				
Time, t	1	2	3	4
Balance, A	14,000	13,550	13,100	12,650

Loan #2				
Time, t	1	2	3	4
Balance, A	14,000	13,440	12,902	12,386

   a. Determine the type of function represented by the data in each table.

   b. Provide an explanation for the type of growth of each function.

   c. Which account has a greater balance after 10 years? after 15 years? Justify your answers.

Chapters 7–9 **Quarterly Standards Based Test** (continued)

4. Order the expressions from least to greatest. Justify your answer. *(HSN-RN.A.1)*

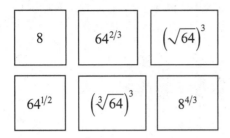

8	$64^{2/3}$	$\left(\sqrt{64}\right)^3$
$64^{1/2}$	$\left(\sqrt[3]{64}\right)^3$	$8^{4/3}$

5. Over a period of 20 years, the daily water consumption C (in ten-thousands of gallons) and the student population P (in thousands) of a college can be modeled by

$$C = \frac{215x - 134.2}{x + 1.6}$$
$$P = 1.2x + 9$$

where x represents the time (in years). Write a model for the daily per capita water consumption D (in gallons per person) as a function of time. *(HSA-APR.D.7)*

6. Choose the correct relationship among the variables in the table. Justify your answer by writing an equation that relates p, q, and r. *(HSA-CED.A.2)*

p	8	-7	-5	1.2
q	6	-5	-10	75
r	12	-17	-7	0.4

   A. The variable q varies inversely with the difference of p and r.

   B. The variable p varies directly with the difference of p and q.

   C. The variable r varies directly with the sum of p and q.

   D. The variable q varies inversely with the sum of p and r.

7. You have bowled 6 games and your average score is 158 points. You think you can score 170 points on each remaining game. How many games do you need to bowl to raise your average game score to 166 points? Justify your answer. *(HSA-REI.A.2)*

Chapters 7–9 **Quarterly Standards Based Test** (continued)

8. The frequencies (in hertz) of the small octave notes on a piano form a geometric sequence. The frequencies of D (labeled "3") and F (labeled "6") are shown in the diagram. What is the approximate frequency of A# (labeled "11")? *(HSF-BF.A.2)*

   A. 220 Hz

   B. 233 Hz

   C. 259 Hz

   D. 315 Hz

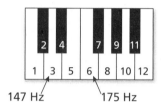

147 Hz   175 Hz

9. You take out a loan for $9000 with an interest rate of 0.375% per month. At the end of each month, you make a payment of $200. *(HSF-LE.A.2)*

   a. Write a recursive rule for the balance a_n of the loan at the beginning of the nth month.

   b. How much do you owe at the beginning of the 14th month?

   c. How long will it take to pay off the loan?

   d. If you pay $300 instead of $200 each month, how long will it take to pay off the loan? How much money will you save? Explain.

10. Order each function from least average rate of change to greatest average rate of change on the interval $1 \le x \le 5$. Justify your answers. *(HSF-IF.B.6)*

   A. $f(x) = 2\sqrt[3]{x-1}$

   B. x and y vary directly, and $y = 4$ when $x = 10$.

   C.
   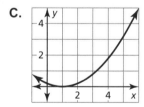

   D.

x	y
1	−2
2	−1
3	0
4	1
5	2

Chapters 7–9 **Quarterly Standards Based Test** (continued)

11. The table shows that the force F (in kilograms) needed to loosen a certain bolt with a wrench depends on the length ℓ (in centimeters) of the wrench's handle. Write an equation that relates ℓ to F. Describe the relationship. *(HSA-CED.A.2)*

Length, ℓ	4	6	8	10
Force, **F**	400	225	125	75

12. Complete the table below for each polynomial function. Then state the possible number of sign changes in the terms of each function. Explain your reasoning. *(HSN-CN.C.9)*

Function	Positive real zeros	Negative real zeros	Imaginary zeros	Total zeros
$f(x)$		2	2	7
$g(x)$		2		3
$h(x)$	4	1		9

13. Classify the solution(s) of each equation as *real numbers*, *imaginary numbers*, or *pure imaginary numbers*. Justify your answers. *(HSN-CN.A.2, HSA-REI.B.4b)*

a. $x^2 + 25 = 0$

b. $2x^2 - 17 = 11$

c. $x^2 = 5x - 4$

d. $x + \sqrt{-9} = 0$

e. $(9 + 7i) - (-4i + 5) = x + 6$

f. $x^2 + x + 8 = 0$

g. $x - \sqrt[3]{-27} = 0$

h. $x^2 + 3x - 5 = 0$

Chapters 7–9 Quarterly Standards Based Test (continued)

14. Which expressions are equivalent to 1? *(HSA-SSE.A.2)*

$\cot x \sec x \sin x$	$\dfrac{\sin(-x)\cot x}{\cos(-x)}$	$\sec^2 x - \tan^2 x$	$\dfrac{\sin\left(\dfrac{\pi}{2} - x\right)}{\cos x}$

15. Which rational expression represents the ratio of the perimeter to the area of the given shape? *(HSA-APR.D.6)*

A. $\dfrac{27}{28x}$

B. $\dfrac{6}{7x}$

C. $\dfrac{9}{14x}$

D. $\dfrac{4}{3x}$

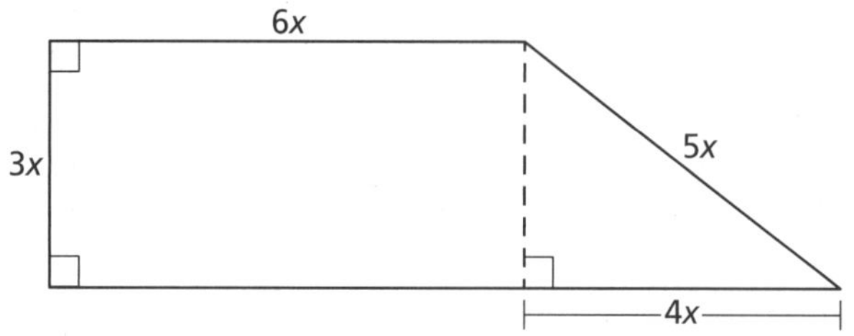

16. The chart shows the depths of water (in feet) at two docks located in an inlet. *(HSS-TF.B.5)*

Time, t	Midnight	2 A.M.	4 A.M.	6 A.M.	8 A.M.	10 A.M.	Noon
Dock #1	2.55 ft	3.8 ft	4.4 ft	3.8 ft	2.55 ft	1.8 ft	2.27 ft
Dock #2	3.18 ft	4.23 ft	4.25 ft	3.21 ft	2.07 ft	1.88 ft	2.81 ft

a. Use a graphing calculator to find trigonometric models for the depth of the water at Dock #1 y_1 and the depth of the water at Dock #2 y_2 as a function of time. Let $t = 0$ represent midnight.

b. Graph the two regression equations in the same coordinate plane on your graphing calculator. Describe the relationship between the graphs.

c. The depth of the water changes with the tide. Which dock is located closer to the mouth of the inlet (where the inlet meets the ocean)? Explain.

Chapters 7–9 Quarterly Standards Based Test (continued)

17. Evaluate each logarithm using $\log_3 2 \approx 0.631$ and $\log_3 5 \approx 1.465$, if necessary. Then order the logarithms by value from least to greatest. *(HSA-SSE.A.2, HSF-LE.A.4)*

   a. $\log 100$ b. $\log_3 10$

   c. $\ln e^3$ d. $\log_3 25$

   e. $\log_3 \dfrac{5}{2}$ f. $\log_3 1$

18. Which function is *not* represented by the graph? *(HSF-BF.B.3)*

   A. $y = 4 \cos x$

   B. $y = 4 \sin\left(\dfrac{\pi}{2} - x\right)$

   C. $y = 4 \sin\left(x - \dfrac{\pi}{2}\right)$

   D. $y = -4 \cos(\pi - x)$

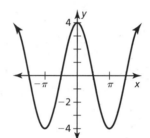

19. Complete each statement with $<$ or $>$ so that each statement is true. *(HSF-TF.A.1, HSF-TF.A.2)*

   a. $\theta \;\square\; 5$ radians

   b. $\cos \theta \;\square\; 0$

   c. $\theta \;\square\; 45°$

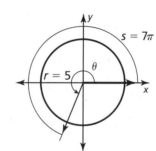

20. Use the Rational Root Theorem and the graph to find all the real zeros of the function $f(x) = 3x^3 - 7x^2 - 2x + 8$. *(HSA-APR.B.3)*

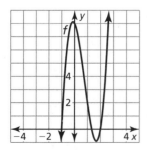

Name _____ Date _____

1. You randomly draw a marble out of a bag containing 4 green marbles, 6 blue marbles, 8 yellow marbles, and 2 red marbles. Find the probability of drawing a marble that is not yellow.

Find $P(\overline{A})$.

2. $P(A) = 0.53$ 3. $P(A) = \frac{4}{7}$ 4. $P(A) = 0.02$

5. You roll a six-sided die 25 times. A 4 is rolled 6 times. What is the theoretical probability of rolling a 4? What is the experimental probability of rolling a 4?

6. Events A and B are independent. Find the missing probability.

   $P(A) = 0.30$

   $P(B) = $ ____

   $P(A \text{ and } B) = 0.08$

7. Events A and B are dependent. Find the missing probability.

   $P(A) = 0.5$

   $P(B \mid A) = 0.35$

   $P(A \text{ and } B) = $ _____

8. Find the probability that a dart thrown at the circular target shown will hit the given region. Assume the dart is equally likely to hit any point inside the target.

   a. the center circle

   b. outside the triangle

   c. inside the triangle but outside the center circle

9. There are 8 men and 12 women working for a company. The company allows its workers to vote between two benefit packages. A total of 5 men and 4 women vote for the first benefit package. Find and interpret the marginal frequencies.

Answers

1. _____

2. _____

3. _____

4. _____

5. _____

   _____

6. _____

7. _____

8. a. _____

   b. _____

   c. _____

9. _____

   _____

   _____

   _____

   _____

   _____

Name_____ Date_____

You roll a die. Find the probability of the event described.   *Answers*

1. You roll a 5.   2. You roll a prime number.

3. You roll a multiple of 2.   4. You roll a number greater than 6.

Evaluate the expression.

5. $_5C_2$ 6. $_7P_3$ 7. $_8C_4$ 8. $_8P_4$

9. You are looking to choose a cable company to provide service at your house. Four companies all offer identical packages at the same price. You have surveyed many people in your neighborhood to find out if they are satisfied with their current cable package that each company produces. The table below shows the results of the survey you conducted. Based on these results, what cable company should you choose?

	Company 1	Company 2	Company 3	Company 4
Satisfied	⫴⫴ ⫴⫴⫴	⫴⫴⫴⫴	⫴⫴⫴⫴ ⫴	⫴⫴⫴⫴
Not Satisfied	⫴⫴⫴	⫴⫴	⫴⫴⫴⫴	⫴⫴

10. For events A and B, $P(A) = \frac{3}{14}$ and $P(B) = \frac{1}{5}$. Also, $P(A \text{ and } B) = \frac{3}{65}$. Are A and B independent events? Explain your answer below.

1. _____
2. _____
3. _____
4. _____
5. _____
6. _____
7. _____
8. _____
9. _____
10. ___See left.___
11. _____
12. _____
13. a._____
    b._____
    c._____

Use the Binomial Theorem to write the 4th term of the binomial expression.

11. $(x + 2y)^6$ 12. $(3x - 2y^2)^8$

13. A game at the state fair has a circular target with a radius of 12 centimeters on a square board measuring 30 centimeters a side, as shown. Players win if they are able to throw a dart and hit the circular area only.

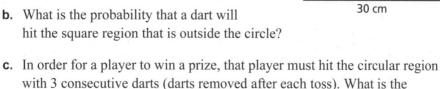

r = 12 cm

30 cm

  a. What is the probability that a dart will hit the circular region?

  b. What is the probability that a dart will hit the square region that is outside the circle?

  c. In order for a player to win a prize, that player must hit the circular region with 3 consecutive darts (darts removed after each toss). What is the probability of a player winning a prize?

Chapter 10 Test A (continued)

14. According to a survey done at your school, about 42% of all the female students participate in 2 sport seasons. You randomly ask 5 female students at your school how many sport seasons they participate in.

a. Draw a histogram of the Binomial distribution for this survey below.

b. What is the most likely outcome to this survey?

c. What is the probability that at least 3 of the 5 female students surveyed participate in 2 sport seasons?

15. Consider a shuffled set of 52 playing cards. The kind of cards that are in the set is listed in the table below.

	Ace	King	Queen	Jack	Non-face card
Black	2	2	2	2	18
Red	2	2	2	2	18

a. You choose one card at random from the shuffled deck. Find the probability that you choose a black card or a jack.

b. You choose one card at random, do not replace it, and then choose a second card at random. Find the probability that you choose a non-face card followed by a queen.

16. There are 15 students (including you) in your Student Council activity. Your closest friends in the activity are Rachel and Randall. Three students must be picked by your teacher of the activity.

a. What is the probability that you, Rachel, and Randall are picked by the teacher?

b. The first student chosen will become the President, the second student chosen will become the Vice President, and the third student chosen will become the Treasurer. What is the probability that you will be picked as the President, Rachel will be picked as the Vice President, and Randall will be picked as the Treasurer?

Answers

14. a. __See left.__

b._____

c._____

15. a._____

b._____

16. a._____

b._____

Name_____ Date _____

You spin a spinner that has equal spots numbered 1–8. Find the probability of the event described.

Answers

1. You spin a 4.   2. You spin a composite number.

3. You spin a multiple of 2.   4. You spin a number less than 1.

Evaluate the expression.

5. $_{12}P_5$ 6. $_7C_4$ 7. $_{13}C_7$ 8. $_9P_4$

9. You are researching a method to determine what will give you the best chance of passing your driver's test. All 3 options for passing the test will cost you the same amount of money. You ask all your friends who have been involved in one of these 3 options. The table shows the results of your research. Based on this information, what method will give you the best chance to pass the driver's test?

	Passed	Not Passed
Book Class	18	6
Driver's School	31	11
Internet Class	8	3

10. Is it possible to use the formula $P(A \text{ and } B) = P(B) \cdot P(A \mid B)$? Explain your reasoning below.

1. _____

2. _____

3. _____

4. _____

5. _____

6. _____

7. _____

8. _____

9. _____

10. ___See left.___

11. _____

12. _____

13. a._____

    b._____

    c._____

Use the Binomial Theorem to write the 5th term of the binomial expression.

11. $(2y - 5)^9$ 12. $(x + 3y^2)^{11}$

13. You are playing a game similar to shuffleboard, where you need to slide a puck into the light gray area of the board in order to score points. The board is surrounded by wood boards that keep the puck in the playing surface. An image of the board and its dimensions are shown to the right.

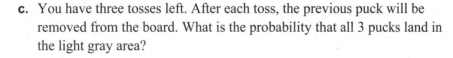

4 feet   1.5 feet

12 feet

5 feet

a. What is the probability that you slide the puck into the light gray area?

b. What is the probability that you slide the puck into the dark gray area?

c. You have three tosses left. After each toss, the previous puck will be removed from the board. What is the probability that all 3 pucks land in the light gray area?

Chapter 10 **Test B** (continued)

14. According to a survey, about 53% of all teenagers under the age of 13 now own a cell phone. You ask 7 randomly chosen teenagers under the age of 13 whether they currently own a cell phone.

   a. Draw a histogram of the Binomial distribution for this survey below.

   b. What is the most likely outcome to this survey?

   c. What is the probability that at least 4 out of 7 teenagers under the age of 13 own a cell phone?

15. A small bag contains 6 pennies, 5 nickels, 3 dimes, 5 quarters, and 2 one-dollar coins.

   a. You choose one coin at random from the bag. What is the probability that you choose a one-dollar coin or a dime?

   b. You choose one coin at random, replace it, and then choose a second coin at random. What is the probability that you first choose a nickel and then choose a penny?

   c. You choose one coin at random, do not replace it, and then choose a second coin at random. What is the probability that you choose a quarter followed by another quarter?

16. While at a family reunion, you are blindfolded to play a game called "tag." In this game, the person who is blindfolded must tag 3 people before their turn has ended. There are 21 people playing the game, including you, your sister, your brother, and your friend.

   a. What is the probability that while you are blindfolded, you tag your sister, brother, and friend?

   b. The first person tagged will become the "goat," the second person tagged will be the "donkey," and the last person tagged will become the "sheep" in the game. What is the probability that you tag your sister as the "goat," your brother as the "donkey," and your friend as the "sheep?"

Answers

14. a. ___See left.___

   b. _____

   c. _____

15. a. _____

   b. _____

   c. _____

16. a. _____

   b. _____

Chapter 10 Alternative Assessment

1. For a carnival game, a turn consists of spinning the spinner shown twice. If the product of the two numbers is odd, you win. If the product of the two numbers is even, you lose. In addition, if the product of the two numbers is prime, you win a grand prize. The assistant assures you that the odds are in your favor because you are more likely to land on an odd number.

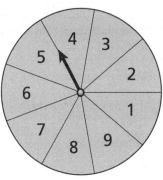

  a. Are you more likely to land on an odd or even number? Explain. Does this imply you are more likely to win on your turn? Explain.

  b. Are the two spins independent or dependent events? Explain.

  c. How many possible outcomes (consisting of two spins) are there?

  d. List the sample space of possible outcomes.

  e. What is the probability of the product of the two numbers being odd?

  f. What is the probability of the product of the two numbers being even?

  g. Is this a fair game? Explain.

  h. Describe one possible grand prize turn. What can you say about the values of the two spins?

  i. Suppose you have a grand prize turn with the first spin landing on 1 and the second spin landing on a prime. Using area, what is the probability of this grand prize turn? Now, suppose you have a grand prize turn with the first spin landing on a prime and the second spin landing on a 1, what is the probability of this grand prize turn? Using what you know about disjoint events, what is the probability of winning the grand prize? Verify this using your sample space.

  j. How could you change the rules of this game to make it more fair?

  k. Using the original rules, how could you change the board of this game to make it more fair?

Name _____ Date _____

Score	Conceptual Understanding	Mathematical Skills	Work Habits
4	Shows complete understanding of: • independent and dependent events • probability and sample space	All answers are correct and explanations are correct and thorough.	Answers all parts of all problems Answers are explained thoroughly with mathematical terminology. Work is very neat and well organized.
3	Shows nearly complete understanding of: • independent and dependent events • probability and sample space	One answer is incorrect but all explanations show correct reasoning and are thorough.	Answers most parts of all problems Answers are explained with mathematical terminology. Work is neat and organized.
2	Shows some understanding of: • independent and dependent events • probability and sample space	Two to three answers are incorrect. Explanations may show incorrect reasoning but are still complete.	Answers some parts of all problems Answers are poorly or incorrectly explained. Work is not very neat or organized.
1	Shows little understanding of: • independent and dependent events • probability and sample space	Four or more answers are incorrect, and explanations are completely incorrect or missing.	Attempts few parts of any problem No explanation is included with answers. Work is sloppy and disorganized.

Name_____ Date_____

Chapter 10 **Performance Task**

A New Dartboard

Instructional Overview	
Launch Question	You are a graphic artist working for a company on a new design for the board in the game of darts. You are eager to begin the project, but the team cannot decide on the terms of the game. Everyone agrees that the board should have four colors. But some want the probabilities of hitting each color to be equal, while others want them to be different. You offer to design two boards, one for each group. How do you get started? How creative can you be with your designs?
Summary	Students use geometric probabilities to design two dart boards with different specifications.
Teacher Notes	Students may not be familiar with the design of an old-fashioned dart board, so it may be helpful to have one in the classroom or a picture to share with the students. It also may be helpful to have pictures of different game boards for student reference.
	Students sometimes have preconceived ideas that confuse symmetry with equal probability, and that is one emphasis of this task—that while the two concepts can sometimes occur together, they are not the same and often do not occur together. Encourage students to think of a way to color a symmetrical design that would show a different area ratio for each color. Encourage them to think of a non-symmetrical design that could be colored so that the colors do have an equal amount of area in the design.
Supplies	Handouts, drawing and coloring supplies, different types of paper, cardboard, or poster board (optional)
Mathematical Discourse	What are some common board games? Which ones have the most visually appealing game boards? Why?
Writing/Discussion Prompts	If you were to purchase one of your game boards, which would it be? Why?

Curriculum Content	
CCSSM Content Standards	HSS-CP.1, HSS-MD.5, HSS-MD.6
CCSSM Mathematical Practices	3. Construct viable arguments and critique the reasoning of others. Students must prove that their game boards match the specifications regarding probability and area.

Performance Task (continued)

Rubric

A New Dartboard	Points
Board is based on 4 colors.	**3 points**
For one board, each of the four colors covers the same area of the board, so they have an equal probability of being hit. For the other board, each of the four colors covers a different area of the board, so they do not have an equal probability of being hit.	**10** Both boards satisfy the requirements. **5** One board satisfies the requirements. **1** Neither board satisfies the requirements.
Worksheet questions are answered correctly. 1. *Sample answer:* red, yellow, green, and blue 2. *Sample answer:* The total area of each color must be the same for the equal probability board, and the area for at least 1 color must be unequal for the other board. 3. *Sample answer:* The shape of either board can be symmetric or non-symmetric. The important thing about the shape is that you must be able to calculate the area of each color on the board. 4. *Sample answer:* The sections do not have to have the same shape, but you must be able to calculate the area of each one. 5–6. Answers will vary with each board.	
The explanations for the probabilities on each board are well-written and thoroughly explained using area. The explanations are supported with calculations using geometric probabilities.	**10** The explanations and calculations are correct. **5** Explanations are correct but the calculations are incorrect. **1** Neither the explanations nor the calculations are correct.
Mathematics Practice: 3. Construct viable arguments and critique the reasoning of others.	**2** For demonstration of practice partial credit can be awarded.
Total Points	**25 points**

Chapter 10 Performance Task (continued)

A New Dartboard

You are a graphic artist working for a company on a new design for the board in the game of darts. You are eager to begin the project, but the team cannot decide on the terms of the game. Everyone agrees that the board should have four colors. But some want the probabilities of hitting each color to be equal, while others want them to be different. You offer to design two boards, one for each group. How do you get started? How creative can you be with your designs?

1. What 4 colors will you use for your board? Will it have a theme or a specific name?

2. How will you make sure that all four colors on one board have the same theoretical probability of being hit and that the colors on the other board do not have the same probability of being hit?

3. How will you choose the shape of your boards? What is important about the shape? Does the board with equal color probabilities have to be symmetrical? Does the board with unequal color probabilities have to be non-symmetrical? Explain.

4. How many sections will you have on each board? What is the minimum number of sections? How will you shape the sections of your boards? Do the sections on the board with equal probability need to be the same shape? Why or why not?

5. How will players score points using your board? Will each section be worth the same amount of points?

6. Calculate the probabilities of hitting each color on your board. Use mathematics to show that each color on one board has an equal probability of being hit and that colors on the other board do not have an equal probability of being hit.

Name _____ Date _____

A normal distribution has a mean of 40 and a standard deviation of 8. Find the probability that a randomly selected *x*-value from the distribution is in the given interval.

Answers

1. at least 30   **2.** between 15 and 28   **3.** at most 33

1. _____

2. _____

Determine whether the histogram has a normal distribution.

3. _____

4.

Attendance

Relative frequency

0.5
0.4
0.3
0.2
0.1
0

51–55 56–60 61–65 66–70 71–75 76–80 81–85 86–90 91–95 96–100

Attendance

5.

Math Test

Relative frequency

0.25
0.20
0.15
0.10
0.05
0

51–55 56–60 61–65 66–70 71–75 76–80 81–85 86–90 91–95

Score

4. _____

5. _____

6. _____

   _____

7. _____

8. _____

9. a._____

   b._____

6. A survey of 1423 college students determined their major during their freshman year of college. Identify the population and the sample.

7. A survey of all teachers at a school found that the mean time planning for their classes is 54 minutes a day. Is the mean time a parameter or a statistic?

8. A researcher gave a group of people a trial medication and then had each individual fill out a form as to what benefits and side effects the medication had. Identify the method of data collection.

   _____

   c._____

   _____

   _____

10. _____

9. A restaurant wants to find out about the satisfaction of its customers. It asks each customer to voluntarily fill out a quick survey at the end of his or her meal.

   a. Identify the type of sample described.

   b. Is the sample biased? Explain your reasoning.

   c. Describe a method for selecting a random sample of customers to survey.

10. Determine whether the survey question may be biased or otherwise introduce bias into the survey: "Do you like the taste of our prize-winning coffee?" Explain your reasoning.

Name_____ Date_____

Chapter 11 Test A

1. Researchers are measuring the growth of 20 similar trees. Ten trees are fed with a liquid nitrogen fertilizer and 10 trees are fed with rain water. Is this research topic being investigated through an experiment or observational study?

2. A national restaurant chain's owners are trying to decide whether they want to open up a franchise in your town. To help them make this decision, they want to find out how often people in your town go out to eat. A researcher interviews people as they leave a local restaurant.

    a. What is the sampling method being used?

    b. Is this a biased or unbiased sample?

3. You want to survey 250 students in your school who took the SAT test this year. You give each of the 250 students a questionnaire and only use the questionnaires that are returned. What type of sampling method did you use?

4. The 40-yard dash times for all football players in the United States are normally distributed with a mean of 5.3 seconds and a standard deviation of 0.3 second. Are these numerical values parameters or statistics?

5. A researcher wants to test the effectiveness of a new medication designed to help dissolve blood clots. The following statement describes the experimental design:

    The researcher is given 400 patients who have blood clots in their legs. Two-hundred patients with the lowest number of blood clots are given the medication, and the other 200 patients are given a placebo. After one month, the patients are evaluated.

    a. Identify a potential problem, if any, with the experimental design.

    b. Describe how you could improve the potential problem, if any, with the experimental design.

A normal distribution has a mean of 122 and a standard deviation of 6. Find the probability that a randomly selected *x*-value from the distribution is in the given interval.

6. between 110 and 128

7. at most 128

8. less than 116

9. at least 116

10. greater than 134

Answers

1. _____

2. a._____

   b._____

3. _____

4. _____

5. a._____

   _____

   _____

   b._____

   _____

   _____

6. _____

7. _____

8. _____

9. _____

10. _____

Chapter 11 **Test A** (continued)

11. A randomized comparative experiment tests whether a muscle supplement increases human muscle density (grams/milliliter). The control group has 10 people and the treatment group, which receives the muscle supplement, has 10 people. The tables show the results.

	Muscle Density (g/mL)				
Control Group	1.06	1.2	1.03	0.97	1.11
Treatment Group	1.2	1.11	1.02	1.16	1.2

	Muscle Density (g/mL)				
Control Group	1.09	1.17	1.12	1.2	1.08
Treatment Group	1.3	1.27	1.2	1.13	1.07

a. Find the mean yields of the control group, $\overline{X}_{control}$, and the treatment group, $\overline{X}_{treatment}$.

b. Find the experimental difference of the means, $\overline{X}_{treatment} - \overline{X}_{control}$.

c. Display the data in a double dot plot below.

12. In a recent survey of 2200 randomly selected U.S. teenagers, 92% said they had a cell phone.

a. Identify the population and the sample.

b. Find the margin of error for the survey.

c. Give an interval that is likely to contain the exact percent of U.S. teenagers who have a cell phone with 95% certainty.

d. You survey 200 teenagers at your school. The results are shown in the graph at the right. Which survey would you use to estimate the percent of U.S. teenagers who have a cell phone? Explain your answer below.

U.S. Teenagers Who Own a Cell Phone

No 16%

Yes 84%

Answers

11. a. _____

_____

b. _____

c. __See left.__

12. a. _____

_____

b. _____

c. _____

d. __See left.__

Chapter 11 Test B

Answers

1. Candy bar researchers want to know whether more teenagers or adults buy their product. Is this research topic best investigated through an experiment or observational study?

2. Your local movie theatre is looking at adding a matinee to their weekend movie schedules. To help them make a decision on this, they want to find out how many people would attend this matinee movie. A researcher makes phone calls to random members in your town.

    a. What is the sampling method being used?

    b. Is this a biased or unbiased sample?

3. Your school is holding voting for the president of your class. You randomly selected five students from every homeroom class. What type of sampling method did you use?

4. The wait times for all customers from 11 A.M. – 3 P.M. at your local bank are normally distributed with a mean of 4.7 minutes and a standard deviation of 3 minutes. Are these numerical values parameters or statistics?

5. A researcher wants to test the effectiveness of a new vaccine used to help resist pneumonia. The following statement describes the experimental design:

    The researcher is given 8 people who will be a part of this experiment. Four people are given the pneumonia vaccine and the other four are assigned the placebo. After 6 months, the members of the study are re-evaluated.

    a. Identify a potential problem, if any, with the experimental design.

    b. Describe how you could improve the potential problem, if any, with the experimental design.

1. _____

2. a._____

   b._____

3. _____

4. _____

5. a._____

   _____

   _____

   _____

   b._____

   _____

   _____

6. _____

7. _____

8. _____

9. _____

10. _____

A normal distribution has a mean of 35 and a standard deviation of 3. Find the probability that a randomly selected x-value from the distribution is in the given interval.

6. greater than 32

7. at most 32

8. at least 41

9. between 29 and 38

10. less than 38

Chapter 11 Test B (continued)

11. A randomized comparative experiment tests whether a hair growth supplement increases the human hair growth rate (in centimeters). The control group has nine people and the treatment group, which receives the hair supplement, has nine people. The table below shows the results. Round your answers to the nearest hundredth, if necessary.

Hair Growth (cm)									
Control Group	12.1	13.2	11.9	14.3	14.1	12.7	13.5	11.9	13.7
Treatment Group	15.2	17.1	18.3	17.6	18.8	16.8	15.9	17.3	17.5

a. Find the mean yields of the control group, $\overline{X}_{control}$, and the treatment group, $\overline{X}_{treatment}$.

b. Find the experimental difference of the means, $\overline{X}_{treatment} - \overline{X}_{control}$.

c. Display the data in a double dot plot below.

12. In a recent survey of 3500 randomly selected U.S. drivers, 62% said they had received at least one speeding ticket.

a. Identify the population and the sample.

b. Find the margin of error for the survey.

c. Give an interval that is likely to contain the exact percent of U.S. drivers who have received at least one speeding ticket with 95% certainty.

d. You survey 50 drivers at your school. The results are shown in the graph at the right. Which survey would you use to estimate the percent of U.S. drivers who have received at least one speeding ticket? Explain your answer below.

U.S. Drivers Who Have Received at Least One Speeding Ticket

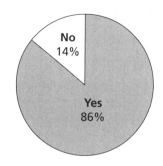

No 14%

Yes 86%

Name_____ Date_____

 Chapter 11 **Alternative Assessment**

1. Your school leaders are considering a change of venue for this year's Junior/Senior Prom. They have tasked the student council with gathering information from the student body regarding the issue. Because 1740 students are enrolled at your school, the council decides to survey a sample of students. Your school has 430 freshmen, 441 sophomores, 427 juniors, and 442 seniors.

   a. One student council member suggests surveying students during the first lunch period by interviewing every fourth student. There are 4 lunch periods, and each one has 435 total students drawn from all grade levels, freshman through senior. Identify the type of sample described. Then tell whether the sample is biased. Explain your reasoning.

   b. Another student suggests waiting until class meetings and randomly selecting 50 juniors and 50 seniors from their meetings for the interview. Identify the type of sample described. Then tell whether the sample is biased. Explain your reasoning.

   c. Describe how the student council might use cluster sampling to gather data.

   d. How many students will be surveyed using the method described in part (a) assuming that all students are present for lunch? Calculate the margin of error for a sample of this size. Is it acceptable?

   e. Calculate the margin of error for the sample described in part (b). Is it acceptable?

   f. The student council would like the survey to have a margin of error of no more than ±2% and include no more than one quarter of the student body. Is this possible? If not, explain why and find the least margin of error (to the nearest percent) that can be achieved by surveying one quarter of the student body.

   g. A random, unbiased survey is agreed upon and administered to 435 students. The results are that 46% of the students want to keep the prom where it is and 54% of the students want to change the venue. From this survey, can the school determine which option the student body prefers? Explain.

Name _____ Date _____

Chapter 11 Alternative Assessment Rubric

Score	Conceptual Understanding	Mathematical Skills	Work Habits
4	Shows complete understanding of: • sampling techniques • sample and survey bias • margins of error	All answers are correct and the explanations are correct and thorough.	Answers all parts of all problems The answers are explained thoroughly with mathematical terminology. Work is very neat and well organized
3	Shows nearly complete understanding of: • sampling techniques • sample and survey bias • margins of error	One answer is incorrect but all explanations show correct reasoning and are thorough.	Answers most parts of all problems The answers are explained with mathematical terminology. Work is neat and organized
2	Shows some understanding of: • sampling techniques • sample and survey bias • margins of error	Two to three answers are incorrect. The explanations may show incorrect reasoning but are still complete.	Answers some parts of all problems The answers are poorly or incorrectly explained. Work is not very neat or organized
1	Shows little understanding of: • sampling techniques • sample and survey bias • margins of error	Four or more answers are incorrect, and the explanations are completely incorrect or missing.	Attempts few parts of any problem No explanation is included with the answers. Work is sloppy and disorganized

Name_____ Date _____

Curving the Test

Instructional Overview	
Launch Question	Test scores are sometimes curved for different reasons using different techniques. Curving began with the assumption that a good test would result in scores that were normally distributed about a C average. Is this assumption valid? Are test scores in your class normally distributed? If not, how are they distributed? Which curving algorithms preserve the distribution and which algorithms change it?
Summary	Students explore arguments for and against curving a test as well as when a curve would be appropriate. Then they calculate and examine the distribution and statistical measures based on test scores before and after adding a constant value to all data points. The distribution of a data set is unchanged by adding a constant to the data points.
Teacher Notes	Encourage students to think objectively about curving a test. Most students are only familiar with a flat curve of adding a constant number of points to each score. They may see the benefits of improving their own grade, but they may not realize that some curves will help grades in certain ranges more than other ranges, offering more points to some students over others. In addition, students may not have thought through the idea of applying a normal distribution to class grades. Would they like to be in a class where the expected grade was a C? Would they like to be in a class in which someone must make an F and someone must make an A+? Encourage them to discuss how outliers affect the principle of curving. Should a curve be applied if one student scores a 100% but the nearest grade is an 80%?
	For a good explanation of other types of curving algorithms, see http://divisbyzero.com/2008/12/22/how-to-curve-an-exam-and-assign-grades/
Supplies	Handouts, calculators
Mathematical Discourse	Have you ever taken a test in which the grades were later curved? Did all students benefit from the curve? What makes a curve fair?
Writing/Discussion Prompts	1. Is it fair to change one student's grade based on the performance of another student? 2. How should a curve affect a class of test scores? What are some characteristics of the data set that the curve should preserve?

Curriculum Content	
CCSSM Content Standards	HSS-ID.1, HSS-ID.2, HSS-ID.3
CCSSM Mathematical Practices	3. Construct viable arguments and critique the reasoning of others: Students must explain circumstances in which curving is appropriate and when it is not.

Chapter 11 **Performance Task** (continued)

Rubric

Curving the Test	Points
1. Students explain responses thoughtfully. *Sample answers:* a. It might be somewhat unfair to curve the test; In this situation, it might be better to give all students 15 additional minutes at the beginning of the next class. b. It would be fair to curve the test; The teacher might add the points for that question to all tests, or omit the question from scoring entirely. c. It might be fair to curve the test; The test may have been too difficult or too lengthy. d. It would be unfair to curve the test; Although this test may have been too easy, it would be unfair to curve down, lowering students' scores. e. It might be fair to curve the test; One possibility would be to have students make corrections to their tests, to reinforce the concepts and help students better understand the material. f. It would be fair to curve the test; The teacher might add the points for that question to all tests, or omit the question from scoring entirely.	**3 points (0.5 point each)**
2. *Sample answer:* Benefits are that grades improve and students are not punished for unfair questions or circumstances; Drawbacks include that some students may feel pressure not to score well so others can have the curve. 3. *Sample answer:* It means that most grades are a C with fewer but the same number of Bs and Ds, and even fewer but the same number of Fs and As; disagree; Test scores for very large groups do tend to be normally distributed, but curving a test for a 30-student class to a normal distribution is not appropriate. If a good test is checking for mastery, most students should show mastery and perform well above a C.	**2 points (1 point each)**

Chapter 11 Rubric (continued)

4. a. 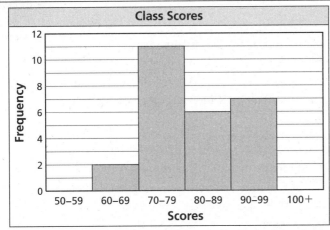 $\mu = 81.85$, median $= 80$, mode $= 75$, range $= 31$, $\sigma = 10$ b. no; The mean is not equal to the median, and the distribution is not symmetric.	**3 points (0.5 point each)**
5. a. Curved data: 75, 70, 72, 69, 72, 94, 74, 94, 77, 85, 76, 77, 85, 74, 100, 83, 81, 91, 98, 90, 77, 97, 91, 81, 99, 98 b. 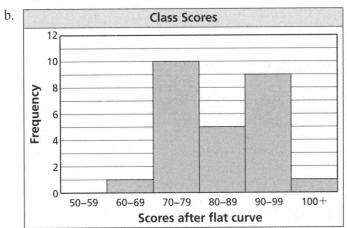 $\mu = 83.85$, median $= 82$, mode $= 77$, range $= 31$, $\sigma = 10$ c. no; The mean is not equal to the median, and the distribution is not symmetric. d. Measures of central tendency, the mean μ, the median, and the mode, increased by the same amount as the curve; Measures of deviation, the standard deviation σ and the range, stayed the same; This is because measures of deviations are based on differences and ratios.	**4 points (0.5 point each)**
Mathematics Practice: Construct viable arguments and critique the reasoning of others.	**2** For demonstration of practice; Partial credit can be awarded.
Total Points	**14 points**

Chapter 11 Performance Task (continued)

Curving the Test

Test scores are sometimes curved for different reasons using different techniques. Curving began with the assumption that a good test would result in scores that were normally distributed about a C average. Is this assumption valid? Are test scores in your class normally distributed? If not, how are they distributed? Which curving algorithms preserve the distribution and which algorithms change it?

Curving a test is a method of converting initial scores to new scores that exhibit a particular characteristic or distribution. There are many methods of curving scores. One is a grade bump in which the teacher adds the same number of points to each test. Other methods involve scaling initial scores so that a certain class average is achieved.

1. Is curving the test appropriate in the following situations? Explain.

   a. A fire drill occurs while students are taking a test. They lose 15 minutes of the period and only 1 student has finished the test at the end of the class.

   b. On a multiple choice test, the teacher inadvertently leaves out the correct answer for one problem.

   c. On a chapter test, no student scores an A.

   d. On a chapter test, all students score an A.

   e. On a chapter test, the teacher expected the average score to be an 80% but was surprised that it was 73% instead.

   f. A problem on the test was poorly worded, making it more difficult to solve.

2. What are the benefits to curving a test? What are some possible drawbacks?

3. Explain what it means for test scores to be normally distributed about a C average. Do you agree or disagree that a good test has a normal distribution about a C average? Explain.

Chapter 11 Performance Task (continued)

4. Use the table.

Class Scores for Chapter 11 Test												
73	68	70	67	70	92	72	92	75	83	74	75	83
72	98	81	79	89	96	88	75	95	89	79	97	96

    a. Make a histogram of the Chapter 11 Test data in the table and calculate μ, the median, the mode, the range, and σ for those scores.

    b. Is this data normally distributed? Why or why not?

5. One curving technique adds a constant number of points to each score. This is sometimes called a *grade bump* or *flat curve*. It can be applied to change the highest or median grade to a certain value or to make up for an unfair or difficult problem.

    a. Apply a flat curve to the initial test score data so that the highest score is a 100. Record the curved scores.

    b. Make a histogram of the curved data and calculate μ, the median, the mode, the range, and σ for the data set.

    c. Is this data normally distributed? Why or why not?

    d. What statistics changed from the original data set? Which ones remained the same? Why?

Chapters 10–11 Quarterly Standards Based Test

1. According to a survey, 37% of American households hire a lawn care service. You randomly select 12 American households to survey. *(HSS-CP.B.9)*

   a. Draw a histogram of the binomial distribution of the number of households out of the 12 you selected that hire a lawn care service.

   b. What is the most likely number of households out of the 12 you selected that hire a lawn care service?

   c. What is the approximate probability that at most 6 households out of the 12 you selected hire a lawn care service? Round your answer to the nearest hundredth.

2. Order the angles from the smallest to largest. Explain your reasoning. *(HSF-TF.A.2)*

   $$\cos \theta_1 = 1$$

   $$\cos \theta_2 = \frac{1}{2}$$

   $$\cos \theta_3 = \frac{\sqrt{3}}{2}$$

   $$\cos \theta_4 = \frac{\sqrt{2}}{2}$$

   $$\cos \theta_5 = \frac{3}{5}$$

   $$\cos \theta_6 = \frac{1}{10}$$

3. You and your friends are ordering a pizza that is made with two cheeses and four toppings. The table below shows the possible choices. How many different pizzas are possible? *(HSS-CP.B.9)*

Cheese	Mozzarella	Romano	Cheddar	Goat	Parmesan
Toppings	Pepperoni	Sausage	Ham	Bacon	Green Pepper
	Pineapple	Onion	Basil	Red Pepper	Mushrooms

Chapters 10–11 **Quarterly Standards Based Test** (continued)

4. Which statements describe the transformations of the graph of $f(x) = x^2 + x$ represented by $g(x) = (3x)^2 + (3x) - 2$? *(HSF-BF.B.3)*

   A. a vertical stretch by a factor of 3

   B. a vertical shrink by a factor of $\frac{1}{3}$

   C. a horizontal shrink by a factor of $\frac{1}{3}$

   D. a horizontal stretch by a factor of 3

   E. a vertical translation 2 units up

   F. a vertical translation 2 units down

   G. a horizontal translation 2 units right

   H. a horizontal translation 2 units left

5. Use the diagram to explain why the equation is true. *(HSS-CP.B.7)*

   $P(A \text{ and } B) = P(B)$

   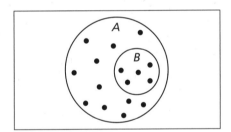

6. Use the sequence $\frac{1}{2}, -\frac{5}{2}, \frac{25}{2}, -\frac{125}{2}, \cdots$ to answer the following.

   a. Describe the pattern.

   b. Write the next term.

   c. Graph the first five terms.

   d. Write a rule for the nth term. *(HSF-IF.A.3)*

Chapters 10–11 **Quarterly Standards Based Test** (continued)

7. A survey asked male and female students about whether they prefer Sign Language class or French class. The table shows the results of the survey. *(HSS-CP.A.4)*

		Class		
		Sign Language	**French**	**Total**
Gender	**Female**		19	
	Male			43
	Total	54		95

   a. Complete the two-way table.

   b. What is the probability that a randomly selected student is male and prefers French class?

   c. What is the probability that a randomly selected female student prefers sign language?

8. Write a system of quadratic inequalities whose solution is represented in the graph. *(HSA-CED.A.2)*

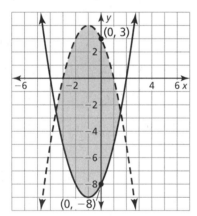

Chapters 10–11 **Quarterly Standards Based Test** (continued)

9. Your friend claims any system formed by three of the following equations will have exactly one solution. *(HSA-REI.C.6)*

| $x + y + z = -1$ | $x - y + z = 4$ | $2x + y + 2z = 1$ |
| $5x - y + 5z = 13$ | $3x - y + z = 2$ | $x + y + 2z = 5$ |

   a. Write a linear system that would support your friend's claim.

   b. Write a linear system that shows your friend's claim is incorrect.

10. Which of the following samples are biased? If the sample is biased, explain why it is biased. *(HSS-IC.A.1)*

   a. A neighborhood homeowners association wants to know whether homeowners are maintaining the upkeep of the roofs of their homes. Each board member surveys three homes on his/her block.

   b. A school cafeteria leaves surveys on the tables for students to fill out. At the end of the lunch period, the school cafeteria collects the filled-out surveys and uses the results.

   c. The owner of a skateboard park wants to know whether the park should remain open on weeknights. Patrons over the age of 40 are randomly selected.

   d. The owner of a frozen yogurt store wants to know whether the store should remain open during the winter months. The cash register randomly chooses which customers to survey as they are making their orders.

11. For all students taking a county-wide Fitness Level Test over a period of five years, the standard deviation was 3.2. During the same five years, a group of 300 students who took the test had a standard deviation of 2.7. Classify each standard deviation as a parameter or a statistic. Explain. *(HSS-IC.A.1)*

Chapters 10–11 **Quarterly Standards Based Test** (continued)

12. A survey asks students about their favorite way to eat popcorn. The results of the survey are displayed in the table shown. *(HSS-IC.B.4, ISS-CP.B.9)*

Survey Results	
Buttered	52%
Caramel	24%
Kettle	17%
Other	7%
(margin of error ±4.2%)	

   a. How many students were surveyed?

   b. Why might the conclusion, "Students generally prefer to eat kettle corn" be inaccurate to draw from this data?

   c. You decide to test the results of the poll by surveying students chosen at random. What is the probability that at least four out of the six students that you survey prefer to eat caramel corn?

   d. Five of the six respondents in your study said that they prefer to eat caramel corn. You conclude that the other survey is inaccurate. Why might this conclusion be incorrect?

   e. What is the margin of error for your survey?

13. Complete the table for the four equations. *(HSF-BF.B.4a)*

Equation	Is the inverse a function?		Is the equation its own inverse?	
	Yes	No	Yes	No
$y = 2^x - 3$				
$y = 5 - x$				
$y = \dfrac{3}{x}$				
$y = x^2 + 4$				

Chapters 10–11 Quarterly Standards Based Test (continued)

14. The normal distribution shown has a mean of 45 and a standard deviation of 6.
    (HSS-ID.A.4)

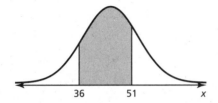

36   51   *x*

   a. Find the percent of the area under the normal curve that is represented by the shaded region.

   b. Describe another interval under the normal curve that has the same area. *(HSS-ID.A.4)*

15. Which of the rational expressions *cannot* be simplified? *(HSA-APR.D.6)*

   A. $\dfrac{2x^2 + 5x - 3}{x^2 - 2x - 15}$

   B. $\dfrac{2x^3 + 2x^2 - 24x}{x^2 - 36}$

   C. $\dfrac{x^3 + 3x^2 - 7x - 21}{x^2 + 5x - 14}$

   D. $\dfrac{x^3 - 8}{x^2 + 2x + 4}$

Name _____ Date _____

In Exercises 1–4, write a rule for g described by the transformations of the graph of f.

Answers

1. $f(x) = 3x$; reflected in the x-axis, then translated 3 units up

1. _____

2. _____

2. $f(x) = x^2$; translated 2 units left, then a vertical shrink by a factor of $\frac{1}{3}$

3. _____

3. $f(x) = \sqrt{x}$; a horizontal stretch by a factor of 5, followed by a reflection in the y-axis

4. _____

5. _____

4. $f(x) = e^x$; translated 2 units right and 3 units down

6. _____

5. The cost of a large pizza is given by $c = 0.50t + 18$, where c is the total cost and t is the number of toppings. The cost of a medium pizza is half the cost of a large pizza with the same number of toppings. Write an equation that represents the cost c of a medium pizza with t toppings.

7. _____

8. a. _____

b. _____

6. Solve the system of linear equations.
   $2x + y = 11$
   $x + y + z = 4$
   $2x + y + z = 9$

9. ___See left.___

10. _____

7. Your cell phone company charges \$0.10 per megabyte of data with a flat fee of \$10. Your friend's company charges \$0.25 per megabyte with no flat fee. If you and your friend paid the same amount for the same number of megabytes, how many megabytes did you each use?

8. The path of a soccer ball can be modeled by the equation $h = -16t^2 + 8t + 3$, where h is the height (in feet) of the soccer ball t seconds after the ball is kicked.

   a. After how many seconds does the ball reach its maximum height?

   b. What is the maximum height of the soccer ball?

9. Graph $y = 2(x - 4)(x + 1)$.

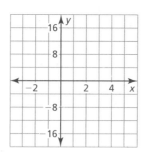

10. Write an equation of the parabola with directrix $x = -1$ and focus $(1, -2)$.

Post Course — Post Course Test (continued)

11. Write the equation of the quadratic function with vertex $(3, -1)$ that passes through the point $(0, 2)$.

12. Write the equation of the quadratic function that passes through the points $(-1, 1)$, $(1, 5)$, and $(2, 10)$.

13. Write an equation of a polynomial function of least degree with rational coefficients and the roots 5 and i.

In Exercises 14–19, solve each equation for x.

14. $x^2 + 7x + 12 = 0$

15. $5(x - 2)^2 = -20$

16. $51 = 4x^4 - 13$

17. $9^{x+6} = 3^{3x}$

18. $\dfrac{5}{2 - x} + \dfrac{4}{x + 2} = \dfrac{9}{2}$

19. $\sqrt[3]{3x + 4} = 7$

20. A population of bacteria grows exponentially over time. The population started with 100 bacteria and after 2 hours there were 225 bacteria. Write an equation that represents the number y of bacteria after x hours.

21. If you invest \$600 at 5% interest compounded continuously, how much would you make after 6 years?

22. Simplify $\dfrac{2}{\sqrt{8}}$.

23. Simplify $\dfrac{2x^2 - 2x - 12}{x - 3}$.

24. Find the roots of $y = 4x^3 + 2x^2 + 2x + 1$.

25. Write $\log_2 9 - 4 \log_2 3$ as single logarithm with a coefficient of 1.

26. What is the domain of $f(x) = \dfrac{3}{2 + x}$?

Answers

11. _____

12. _____

13. _____

14. _____

15. _____

16. _____

17. _____

18. _____

19. _____

20. _____

21. _____

22. _____

23. _____

24. _____

25. _____

26. _____

Post Course Post Course Test (continued)

27. Graph $x + y^2 = 16$.

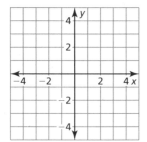

Answers

27. ____See left.____

28. _____

29. _____

30. _____

31. _____

32. _____

33. _____

34. _____

35. ____See left.____

28. Simplify $\dfrac{x^2 + 4x + 3}{x^2 - 1} \div \dfrac{x + 3}{x + 1}$.

29. Simplify $\dfrac{x + 3}{2 - x} + \dfrac{x}{x + 3}$.

30. Compute $\displaystyle\sum_{j=0}^{5}(3j + 2)$.

31. Calculate the sum of the infinite geometric sequence.

$\dfrac{3}{2}, \dfrac{1}{2}, \dfrac{1}{6}, \dfrac{1}{18}, \cdots$

32. Convert $172°$ to radians.

33. Convert $\dfrac{5\pi}{3}$ to degrees.

34. Compute $\cos 690°$.

35. Graph $y = 4\sin\left(x + \dfrac{\pi}{2}\right)$.

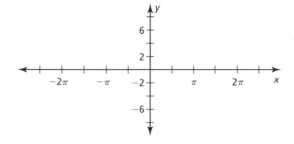

Post Course **Post Course Test** (continued)

36. Write the equation of the sinusoidal.

Answers

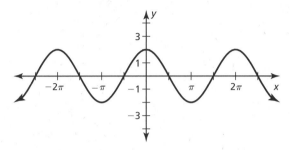

36. _____

37. _____

38. _____

39. _____

40. _____

37. Simplify $\sin(-\theta) \cdot \sec\theta$.   **38.** Compute $\sin 15°$.

41. _____

39. $P(A) = 0.3$, $P(B) = 0.5$, and $P(A \text{ and } B) = 0.15$. What is $P(A \text{ or } B)$?

42. _____

43. _____

40. How many different 5-card hands are possible from a deck of 52 playing cards?

41. A trial drug is 45% effective at fighting a disease. If five people use the drug, what is the probability that the drug will be effective for exactly three of them?

_____

44. _____

45. _____

42. The weights of soup cans are normally distributed with a mean of 8.10 ounces and a standard deviation of 0.15 ounce. What is the probability a can will weigh between 7.8 ounces and 8.25 ounces?

46. _____

47. _____

43. Your high school randomly selects two students from each grade to complete a survey to estimate how many total students at the school would like to join an extracurricular activity. Identify the population and sample.

44. Every fifth bag of potato chips is measured to estimate the average weight of the bags. Identify the type of sampling method used.

45. In a survey of 400 college students, 27% said they had transferred to a new school after 1 year of attendance. Give an interval that is likely to contain the exact percentage of students who transferred to a new school after 1 year of attendance.

46. Compute the experimental difference between the means using the table.

Control	5.1	4.8	5.2	5.0	4.7	4.9	4.8	5.0	4.9	5.1
Treatment	5.1	5.2	4.9	5.4	5.5	5.0	5.0	4.9	5.4	5.3

47. Should you use an observational study or an experiment to determine whether there exists a relationship between the grades of students and the number of older siblings the student has?

Post Course Test Item Analysis

Item Number	Skills
1	transforming graphs of linear functions
2	transforming graphs of quadratic functions
3	transforming graphs of square root functions
4	transforming graphs of exponential functions
5	transforming graphs of linear functions
6	solving systems of linear equations
7	modeling using linear systems
8	finding the vertex of quadratic functions
9	graphing quadratic functions
10	translating between the geometric description and the equation of parabolas
11	constructing quadratic functions given a description
12	constructing quadratic functions given a description
13	constructing a polynomial function given its roots
14	solving quadratic equations by factoring
15	solving quadratic equations with complex solutions
16	solving equations by taking nth roots
17	solving exponential equations

Item Number	Skills
18	solving rational equations
19	solving radical equations
20	constructing exponential models given a description
21	using exponential models
22	rationalizing the denominator of a fraction
23	dividing polynomials
24	finding the roots of a polynomial function
25	applying the rules logarithms
26	identifying the domain of a rational expression
27	graphing parabolas
28	dividing rational expressions
29	adding rational expressions
30	computing summations
31	computing the sum of an infinite geometric sequence
32	converting degrees to radians
33	converting radians to degrees
34	computing the trigonometric ratio of any angle

Item Number	Skills
35	graphing trigonometric functions
36	writing trigonometric functions from graphs
37	applying trigonometric ratios
38	applying angle sum and difference formulas
39	calculating probability
40	counting combinations
41	computing probabilities using binomial distributions

Item Number	Skills
42	finding a normal probability
43	identifying populations and samples
44	identifying sampling methods
45	calculating margin of error
46	evaluating the results of experiments
47	comparing experiments and observational studies

Answers

Prerequisite Skills Test

1. $x = \pm\sqrt{3}$ **2.** $x = -2$ **3.** $x = 4$

4. $x = 5$ **5.** $x = -4, \frac{4}{3}$

6. 5 ft from the center

7. 92   **8.** $y = 0.1x + 3$

9. no real solutions, two imaginary solutions

10. 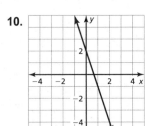   **11.**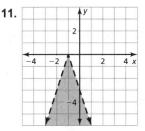

12.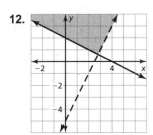

13. $f(3) = 68$ **14.** $y = 0.5x + 8$

15. $y = 25x - 15$ **16.** $g(x) = 7x - 1$

17. $a_n = 6n - 2$ **18.** $(3, 11)$

19. $\left(\frac{2}{3}, 3\right)$ **20.** $(3, 1)$

21. $243x^{10}$ **22.** $\dfrac{x^2}{6y^5}$

23. $\dfrac{103}{118} \approx 87.3\%$ **24.** $\dfrac{103}{120} \approx 85.8\%$

25. \$22.50   **26.** $y = 1000(1.05)^{x-1}$

27.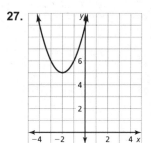

28. 85   **29.** 9.2

30. $-2x^2 + 2x + 7$ **31.** $x^3 + 1$

32. $(1, 6)$ and $(2, 3)$ **33.** 320 in.^{2}

34. $\sqrt[5]{x} + \sqrt[3]{y^5}$ **35.** $x = -7, 3$ **36.** $x = -3, \frac{4}{3}$

37. 120 ft^2

38.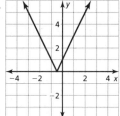

39. $y = -\frac{1}{2}x + 3$

40. a. $x > \frac{7}{5}$ or $x < -1$

     b.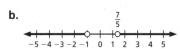

Pre-Course Test

1. $\dfrac{x + 3}{(x + 2)(x - 3)}$ **2.** $\dfrac{x^2 + 5x - 9}{(x - 3)(x + 2)}$

3. 20 ft   **4.** 52 cm

5. translation 1 unit right and a vertical stretch by a factor of 2

6. translation 3 units left and 4 units down

7. horizontal shrink by a factor of $\frac{1}{3}$ and a translation 4 units up

8. reflection in the x-axis and a reflection in the y-axis

Answers

9. $4 = 3x - 5$

10. $(-3, 9)$

11. 4 in.^{2}

12. $(x + 3)(x + 4)$

13. 0.95 sec

14. $y = (x + 4)^2 - 16$

15. $(2, 12)$ and $\left(-\frac{1}{3}, \frac{1}{3}\right)$

16. $a_n = 6(2)^{n-1}$

17. $x = \pm 4$

18.

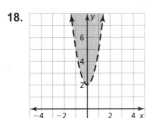

19. $y = 25(x - 16)^2 + 1000$

20. $3, 6, 12, 24, 48$

21. $5, 9, 15, 23, 33$

22.

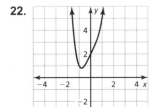

23. $x - 2$

24. $x = -5, -2, 0, 1$

25. $y = 2(x - 1)(x + 1)(x + 3)$

26. $3x^3 y^{8/3}$

27.

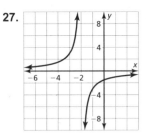

28. $6x^3 + 12x^2$

29. $r = \dfrac{3.5}{t}$

30. $x = 5, -\frac{3}{7}$

31. $x = 4$

32. vertical shrink by a factor of $\frac{1}{2}$, followed by a translation 2 units up

33. 1

34. $\frac{4}{13}$

35. $\frac{1}{10}$

36. 12 two-letter code words

37. about 47.5%

38. $150°$

39. $f^{-1}(x) = x^2 - 2$

40. 1.16096

41. $-x^2 + 5x - 1$

42. stratified sampling method

43. $y = \frac{1}{80}x^2$

44. a. $x \neq -2$

b. $y \neq 0$

45. $-i$

46. $15 + 6i$

47. $-3 < x < -2$

48. $\dfrac{3\sqrt{10}}{10}$

Chapter 1

1.1–1.2 Quiz

1. linear

2. quadratic

3. absolute value

4.

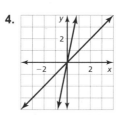

The graph is a vertical stretch by a factor of 5 of the graph of the parent linear function.

5.

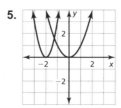

The graph is a vertical stretch by a factor of 3, followed by a translation 2 units left of the graph of the parent quadratic function.

Answers

6.

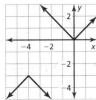

The graph is a reflection in the *x*-axis, followed by a translation 4 units left and 3 units down of the graph of the parent absolute value function.

7. $g(x) = 4x + 9$ **8.** $g(x) = -2|x - 2|$

9. $g(x) = 4x - 4$ **10.** $g(x) = -3|x - 1| - 4$

11. Translate the graph of f 5 units up and then vertically stretch the graph by a factor of $\frac{5}{4}$; $65.94

Test A

1. $y = 3x + 12$; A child grows 3 inches every month.

2. $y = -100x + 700$; Every year, home phone sales decrease by 100 million.

3. $y = 3$; You are walking at a constant rate of 3 miles per hour.

4. $(0, -4, -2)$ **5.** $(-3, 6, -2)$ **6.** no solution

7. infinitely many solutions

8. B; $g(x) = -4x + 5$ **9.** A; $g(x) = 4x - 5$

10. C; $g(x) = -5x + 4$

11. The store used 4 pounds of raisins, 2 pounds of sunflower seeds, and 3 pounds of chocolate-covered peanuts.

12.

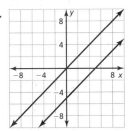

The graph of f is a translation 5 units down of the graph of the parent linear function.

13.

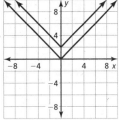

The graph of g is a translation 2 units up of the graph of the parent absolute value function.

14.

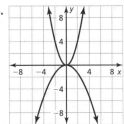

The graph of h is a reflection in the *x*-axis, followed by a vertical shrink by a factor of $\frac{1}{3}$ of the graph of the parent quadratic function.

15. linear; 9 gal **16.** $g(x) = -3|x + 1| - 1$

17. $g(x) = 2x^2 + 6$ **18.** $g(x) = |2x| - 3$

19. $p(s) = \frac{8}{3}s - 20$; This will horizontally shrink the graph by a factor of $\frac{1}{2}$; $780

Test B

1. $y = -\frac{1}{2}x + 1800$; The loan balance decreases by $500 every month.

2. $y = 5x + 20$; The canoe rental increases by 5 dollars for every hour of rental.

3. $y = 6$; The treadmill speed remains constant at 6 miles per hour.

4. $(-1, -6, 1)$ **5.** $(1, 3, 1)$

6. infinitely many solutions

7. no solution **8.** C; $g(x) = -x + 3$

9. B; $g(x) = 3x - 1$ **10.** A; $g(x) = -3x + 1$

11. 6 reserved tickets, 3 field-level tickets, 1 box ticket

Answers

12.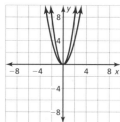

The graph of f is a vertical stretch by a factor of 2 of the graph of the parent quadratic function.

13.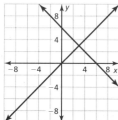

The graph of f is a reflection in the x-axis, followed by a translation 6 units up of the graph of the parent linear function.

14.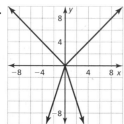

The graph of f is a reflection in the x-axis, followed by a vertical stretch by a factor of 3 of the graph of the parent absolute value function.

15. quadratic; 3 ft

16. $g(x) = -2|x + 1|$ or $g(x) = -2|-x - 1|$

17. $g(x) = 2x + 7$ **18.** $g(x) = 3x^2 + 2$

19. $g(t) = -\frac{7}{2}t^2 + 35t + \frac{3}{2}$; This will vertically shrink the graph by a factor of $\frac{1}{2}$; 85.5 ft

Alternative Assessment

1. a. absolute value function, constant function;
   to $f(x)$: translation 3 units right and 1 unit up;
   to $g(x)$: translation 2 units up

   b. $f(x) = |x - 3| + 1$

   c. $g(x) = 3$

d. $y = |x - 3| + 1$
   $y = 3$

e. $(1, 3)$ and $(5, 3)$ or $x = 1$, $y = 3$ and $x = 5$, $y = 3$

f. Students should substitute the ordered pairs into both functions to verify.

2. a.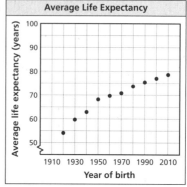

The data show a linear relationship.

b. $y = 0.26x - 433.2$

c. $r = 0.97$; The data show a strong positive linear correlation.

d. 81.9 years; yes

e. 331.8 years; no; The data point is far away from the data used to make the model; It has a greater likelihood of error; The data show a slowing of the growth rate as seen by the average increase of about 3 years per decade between 1920 and 1960, but only half that, an average increase of 1.5 years per decade, between 1960 and 2010.

Chapter 2

2.1–2.2 Quiz

1. The graph of g is a vertical shrink by a factor of $\frac{1}{3}$, followed by a vertical translation 2 units down of the graph of f.

2. The graph of g is a horizontal translation 4 units right and a vertical translation 2 units up of the graph of f.

3. The graph of g is a reflection in the x-axis, followed by a vertical translation 4 units down of the graph of f.

4. $g(x) = -4x^2 - 8$; $(0, -8)$

5. $g(x) = (9x + 34)^2 + 7$; $\left(-3\frac{7}{9}, 7\right)$

Answers

6.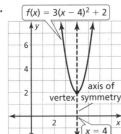

$f(x) = 3(x - 4)^2 + 2$

7.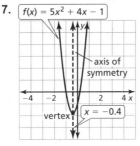

$f(x) = 5x^2 + 4x - 1$

12.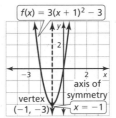

$f(x) = 3(x + 1)^2 - 3$

increasing: $(-1, \infty)$, decreasing: $(-\infty, -1)$

8. $(4, 0), (-2, 0)$; increasing to the left of $x = 1$, decreasing to the right of $x = 1$

9. $(6, 0), (3, 0)$; increasing to the right of $x = 4.5$, decreasing to the left of $x = 4.5$

10. 0.25 sec   **11.** 38 m

13.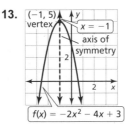

$f(x) = -2x^2 - 4x + 3$

increasing: $(-\infty, -1)$, decreasing: $(-1, \infty)$

Test A

1. $(1, 6)$ **2.** $g(x) = -4x^2 + 12$

3. $g(x) = |x - 1| + 1$

4. focus: $(0, 4)$, directrix: $y = -4$, axis of symmetry: $x = 0$

5. second differences are the same; $f(x) = 2x^2 - 2x - 2$

6. $f(x) = \dfrac{x^2}{4} + 2$ **7.** $x = -\dfrac{y^2}{12}$

8. $f(x) = -\frac{1}{4}x^2 + x + 3$

9. $x = y^2 - 4y + 6$

10. focus: $\left(-\frac{1}{2}, 0\right)$, directrix: $x = \frac{1}{2}$, axis of symmetry: $y = 0$

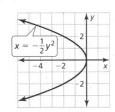

$x = -\frac{1}{2}y^2$

11. 197 ft

14. $x = \frac{1}{32}y^2$ **15.** 36,000 bears

Test B

1. $(2, -7)$ **2.** $g(x) = 9x^2 + 1$

3. $g(x) = -(-x + 1)^2$

4. focus: $(-5, 0)$, directrix: $x = 5$, axis of symmetry: $y = 0$

5. second differences are the same; $f(x) = 3x^2 - 3x - 3$

6. $f(x) = -\dfrac{x^2}{8} + 2$ **7.** $x = -\dfrac{y^2}{8}$

8. $f(x) = 2x^2 + 20x + 52$

9. $x = 6y^2 - 12y + 5$

10. focus: $(0, -3)$, directrix: $y = 3$, axis of symmetry: $x = 0$

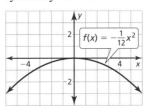

$f(x) = -\frac{1}{12}x^2$

Answers

11. $20

12.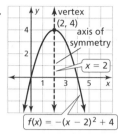

$f(x) = -(x-2)^2 + 4$

increasing: $(-\infty, 2)$, decreasing: $(2, \infty)$

13.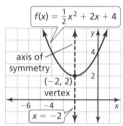

$f(x) = \frac{1}{2}x^2 + 2x + 4$

increasing: $(-2, \infty)$, decreasing: $(-\infty, -2)$

14. $f(x) = -\dfrac{x^2}{16} + 3$ **15.** 89 spotted trout

Alternative Assessment

1. minimums: a, c, e, f; maximums: b, d; same vertex: b, d, and f have vertex of $(-1, -2)$; same range: a and f have range of $y \geq -2$, b and d have range of $y \leq -2$, c and e have range of $y \geq -4$

2. a. vertical shrink

   b. The distance between the vertex and electronics located at the focus gets larger; For a vertical shrink, the coefficient a is getting smaller. So, its denominator, which is a multiple of p, is getting larger.

   c. Answers will have a values whose absolute values are smaller than $\frac{1}{8}$;

     Sample answer: $y = \frac{1}{16}x^2$

3. a. yes; His best height is about 3.9 feet, which is 46.8 inches.

   b. We are discussing a maximum height, so the parabola must open down.

Chapter 3

3.1–3.3 Quiz

1. $x = 4, x = -3$ **2.** $x = 4, x = 0.5$

3. $x = 2, x = 3$

4. $x = \dfrac{3 + \sqrt{5}}{2}, x = \dfrac{3 - \sqrt{5}}{2}$

5. $x = \dfrac{1 + \sqrt{13}}{2}, x = \dfrac{1 - \sqrt{13}}{2}$

6. $x = \dfrac{2 + \sqrt{14}}{2}, x = \dfrac{2 - \sqrt{14}}{2}$

7. $x = 6, y = 8$

8. $-3 + 6i$ **9.** $3 + 9i$

10. $x = \dfrac{i\sqrt{10}}{5}, x = \dfrac{-i\sqrt{10}}{5}$

11. $x = \sqrt{86} - 8, x = -\sqrt{86} - 8$

12. $x = 6 + \sqrt{10}, x = 6 - \sqrt{10}$

13. $y = (x + 2)^2 - 9; (-2, -9)$

14. a. 69 ft   **b.** 4.3 sec   **c.** 105 ft

15. 3 ft

Test A

1. $x = -10, x = -6$ **2.** $x = -5, x = 9$

3. $x = \frac{1}{2}, x = 1$ **4.** $x = -5, x = -\frac{7}{3}$

5. $x = \pm\frac{2}{7}i$ **6.** $x = \pm 3$

7. two real solutions   **8.** one real solution

9. no real solutions   **10.** two real solutions

11. a. 10.54 sec   **b.** 1632 ft

12. $2 - 7i$ **13.** $-15 - 21i$

14. $(-5, -56), (-1, -8)$ **15.** no solution

16.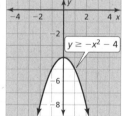

$y \geq -x^2 - 4$

Answers

17.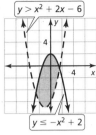

$y > x^2 + 2x - 6$

$y \le -x^2 + 2$

18. 15 sec

19. 14.4 in., 21.6 in.

20. $25 < x < 50$

Test B

1. $x = -5, x = -7$

2. $x = \pm 4$

3. $x = -13, x = 3$

4. $x = -\dfrac{5}{6} \pm \dfrac{i\sqrt{35}}{6}$

5. $x = -2, x = \dfrac{5}{4}$

6. $x = \pm\dfrac{7}{6}i$

7. two real solutions

8. one real solution

9. no real solutions

10. two real solutions

11. 256 ft

12. $-3 + 4i$

13. $-15 + 29i$

14. $(-3, 19), (1, 3)$

15. no solution

16.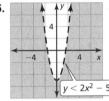

$y < 2x^2 - 5$

17.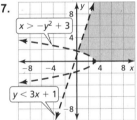

$x > -y^2 + 3$

$y < 3x + 1$

18. $500

19. small base = 13 yd, larger base = 17 yd

20. $0.098 < t < 1.28$

Alternative Assessment

1. The functions could have a different vertex with either a vertical shrink or stretch to have the same x-intercepts. Or, the functions could open in opposite directions; a, c, e, and f have zeros of $x = -3$ and $x = 1$.

2. a.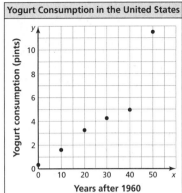

Yogurt Consumption in the United States

Define x to be the number of years after 1960; The function increases but not at a constant rate. The change is slower at first and then increases more quickly.

b. $y = 0.004x^2 - 0.012x + 0.9$

c. $R^2 = 0.92; (40, 4.95);$ The year 2000 $(40, 4.95)$ does not follow quadratic growth.

d. no; The average yogurt consumption was never 0. So, people were always eating some amount of yogurt.

e. 14.6 lbs

f. *Sample answer:* Yogurt consumption increased only slightly between 1990 and 2000, but then more than doubled in the 2000s; milk prices, advertising, new kinds of yogurt; Milk prices could have been high in the 1990s, raising the price of yogurt and discouraging people to buy it. The advertising of yogurt could have improved. Greek yogurt was introduced in the 2000s, starting a huge growth trend.

Quarterly Standards Based Test

1. B
2. A
3. D

4. a. $g(x) = -3x^2 + 2$

b. $g(x) = \dfrac{1}{5}(x + 2)^2 - \dfrac{1}{5}$

c $g(x) = -|4x| + 4$

d. $g(x) = 4(x + 3) - 7$

5. B
6. C

Answers

7. a. Check students' work.

b. $y = 23.6x + 74.67$; about 641 bait fish

c. Initially there were 75 bait fish in the tank. About 24 bait fish are added to the tank each minute.

d. no; Data is only given for times of 0 to 5 seconds, so it is not reasonable to extrapolate so far beyond the domain of the data. It would take a big tank to hold that many bait fish.

8. $y = -0.87x + 5.05$; $r = -0.918$; r is close to -1, so the points lie close to a line with a negative slope.

9. $(0, 3, 4)$

10. $<$; The vertex of your serve is $(1, 4)$. So, the ball reaches a maximum height of 4 feet. Your friend's serve reaches a maximum height of 6 feet.

11. a. \$1.50   **b.** \$1.40   **c.** \$15

12. d, a, b, c   **13.** B and D

14. *Sample answer:* $f(x) = -4(x - 2) + \frac{1}{2}$

15. a. Basic Cable Company A: $y = 30x + 75$,
Basic Cable Company B: $y = 40x$

b. Basic Cable Company B is more economical for the first 7.5 months.

c. new equation: $y = 30x + 30$; The graph of the equation has been translated 45 units down, which shows that the set up fee was lowered from \$75 to \$30. Basic Cable Company B is more economical for only the first 2.5 months.

16. A

17. a. constant; The graph of g is a vertical translation 6 units up of the graph of the parent constant function.

b. quadratic; The graph of h is a vertical translation 5 units up of the graph of the parent quadratic function.

c. linear; *Sample answer:* The graph of h is a vertical translation 9 units down of the graph of the parent linear function.

d. absolute value; The graph of g is a vertical shrink by a factor of $\frac{1}{3}$, followed by a translation 1 unit right and 4 units up of the graph of the parent absolute value function.

e. quadratic; The graph of g is a reflection in the x-axis, followed by translations 6 units left and 5 units down of the graph of the parent quadratic function.

f. linear; The graph of h is a vertical stretch by a factor of 3 and a vertical translation 7 units down of the graph of the parent linear function.

18. $y > 0.05x^2 - x + 7.5$; $y < 0.01x^2 - 0.2x + 6$

19. your claim: $y = 2x^2 - 8x + 7$;
your friend's claim: $y = 2x^2 - 8x + 9$

20. 2, 6   **21.** C

Chapter 4

4.1–4.4 Quiz

1. polynomial function,
$f(x) = 3x^4 + 4x^2 - 5x - 10$, degree 4, quartic, leading coefficient 3

2. not a polynomial function

3. a. increasing: $x > 3$, decreasing: $x < 3$

b. $x < 2, x > 4$

c. $2 < x < 4$

4. perimeter: $8x + 2$, area: $3x^2 + 3x - 2$

5. $2x^3 + 4x^2 - 28x + 24$

6. $x^2 - 6x + 2$

7. $x^5 + 10x^4 + 40x^3 + 80x^2 + 80x + 32$

8. $(3x - 11) + \dfrac{28x + 30}{x^2 + 3x + 3}$

9. $4(a - 1)(a - 2)$

10. $5(x^2 + 4)(x + 2)(x - 2)$

11. $(z - 1)(2z^2 - z + 3)$

12. $f(-3) = 0$; $f(x) = 3x^2(x - 4)(x + 3)$

Answers

13. $0 \le x \le 1.5$; All three factors of V represent physical lengths, so they cannot be negative.

Test A

1. $x^4 - x^3 - 5x^2 + 3x + 6$

2. $x^4 - x^3 - 2x^2 - 4x - 24$

3. $3x^2 + 15x + 40 + \dfrac{132}{x - 3}$

4. $27x^3 - 54x^2 + 36x - 8$

5. $m^3 - 7m + 6$

6. $2x^2 - 4x + 3 + \dfrac{5x - 5}{x^2 + 2x + 2}$

7. $25x^2 + 30x + 9$

8. $z^7 - 2z^6 + 5z^5 - 2z^2 + 4z - 10$

9. a. $f(x)$ has one distinct zero at 0, with a multiplicity of 3.

$g(x)$ has one distinct zero at -2, with a multiplicity of 3.

   b. The graph of g is a translation 2 units left of the graph of f.

   c. increasing for $-\infty < x < \infty$

10. a. Using the Remainder Theorem, $V(-2) = 42$ is not zero, so $(x + 2)$ is not a factor of V.

   b. Because $x = -4$ would be the zero of $x + 4$, use the Remainder Theorem to show that $V(-4) = 0$, making $x + 4$ a factor;

$V(x) = (x - 5)(x + 4)(x - 1)$

11. a. $A(t) = 27t^4 - 30t^3 + 10t^2 - 50t + 1600$

   b. neither; $f(-x) \ne f(x)$ and $f(-x) \ne -f(x)$

12. $p(t) = t^3 - 2t^2 + 3t + 5$; \$835

13. degree is 3 (cubic), leading coefficient is 1

14. $W(x) = 2304\pi x^3$;

$W(5) = 288{,}000\pi \approx 904{,}779$ in.^{3}

Test B

1. $x^4 + 3x^3 + 3x^2 + 3x + 2$

2. $x^4 + x^3 - 25x^2 - 5x + 100$

3. $4x^2 - 8x + 4$

4. $c^{10} - 4c^9 - 2c^8 - 6c^2 + 24c + 12$

5. $4x^2 + 36x + 156 + \dfrac{608}{x - 4}$

6. $b^3 + 8b^2 + 21b + 18$

7. $3x^2 + 7x + 18 + \dfrac{52x - 21}{x^2 - 3x + 1}$

8. $27x^3 + 27x^2 + 9x + 1$

9. a. $f(x)$ has one zero at 0, with a multiplicity of 4.

$g(x)$ has one zero at -4, with a multiplicity of 4.

   b. The graph of g is a translation 4 units left of the graph of f.

   c. decreasing for $x < -4$, increasing for $x > -4$

10. a. Using the Remainder Theorem, $V(-5) = -360$ is not equal to zero.

   b. Because $x = -2$ would be the zero of $x + 2$, use the Remainder Theorem to show that $V(-4) = 0$, making $x + 2$ a factor;

$V(x) = (x - 7)(x - 5)(x + 2)$

11. $p(t) = 2t^3 - 4t^2 + t + 2$; \$2894

12. degree is 3 (cubic), leading coefficient is 1

13. a. $A(t) = 9t^4 + 3t^2 + 105$

   b. even; $f(-t) = f(t)$

14. $W(x) = 3x^2 - 3x$; $W(15) = 630$ ft

Answers

Alternative Assessment

1. a. *Sample answer:* $(2x + 5)(2x - 5) = 4x^2 - 25$

    b. *Sample answer:*
$$(x + 5)(x - 2) = x^2 + 3x - 10$$

    c. *Sample answer:*
$$(x^2 + 1)(x - 2) \text{ or } (x + y)(x - z);$$
$$(x^2 + 1)(x - 2) = x^3 - 2x^2 + x - 2 \text{ or}$$
$$(x + y)(x - z) = x^2 - xz + xy - yz$$

2. a.

$$\left(x^3\right)^2 - \left(y^3\right)^2 = \left(x^3 - y^3\right)\left(x^3 + y^3\right)$$
$$= (x - y)\left(x^2 + xy + y^2\right)(x + y)\left(x^2 - xy + y^2\right)$$

    b.

$$\left(x^2\right)^3 - \left(y^2\right)^3 = \left(x^2 - y^2\right)\left(\left(x^2\right)^2 + x^2y^2 + \left(y^2\right)^2\right)$$
$$= (x - y)(x + y)\left(x^4 + x^2y^2 + y^4\right)$$

    c. Set the results from part (a) and part (b) equal to each other. Common terms cancel out.

$$\left(x^3\right)^2 - \left(y^3\right)^2 = \left(x^2\right)^3 - \left(y^2\right)^3;$$
$$\cancel{(x - y)}\left(x^2 + xy + y^2\right)\cancel{(x + y)}\left(x^2 - xy + y^2\right)$$
$$= \cancel{(x - y)}\,\cancel{(x + y)}\left(x^4 + x^2y^2 + y^4\right)$$

3. a. Let $x =$ the first number: $(x)(x + 1)(x + 2)$;

    Let $x =$ the second number: $(x - 1)(x)(x + 1)$;

    Let $x =$ the third number: $(x - 2)(x - 1)(x)$

    b. $x^3 + 3x^2 + 2x - 336 = 0$; $x^3 - x - 336 = 0$;
$$x^3 - 3x^2 + 2x - 336 = 0$$

    c. $x = 6$, numbers are 6, 7, 8; $x = 7$, numbers are 6, 7, 8; $x = 8$, numbers are 6, 7, 8

    d. *Sample answer:* guess and check, prime factorization

Chapter 5

5.1–5.3 Quiz

1. ± 2 **2.** -5

3. a. 125   **b.** 64

4. $x = 4$ **5.** $x = -1.32$ **6.** $8^{3/5}$

---

7. $500^{1/3}$ **8.** $\dfrac{8 + \sqrt{2}}{62}$ **9.** $5m^{5/2}$

10. $\dfrac{3}{x^{2/3}}$ **11.** $5bn^{1/5}$

12. The graph of g is a translation 2 units right of the graph of the parent function; $g(x) = \sqrt{x - 2}$

13. The graph of g is a translation 2 units left and 1 unit down of the graph of the parent function;
$$g(x) = \sqrt{x + 2} - 1$$

14. vertex: $(2, 0)$, parabola opens right

15. a. 4.94 in.

     b. 2.46 in.

Test A

1. 16   **2.** 2   **3.** $2yz\sqrt[5]{xy}$

4. 25   **5.** $2\sqrt{5}$ **6.** $\dfrac{-1 + \sqrt{3}}{2}$

7. $g(x) = \sqrt{x} - 2$ **8.** $g(x) = -\sqrt[3]{x}$

9. $g(x) = 3\sqrt[5]{x - 1}$ **10.** $g(x) = 2\sqrt{x + 2} - 3$

11. 35.97 mi/h

12. $(f + g)(x) = x^{5/3}$, all real numbers;
$$(f - g)(x) = 5x^{5/3}, \text{ all real numbers;}$$
$$(f + g)(-8) = -32; \ (f - g)(-8) = -160$$

13. $(f \bullet g)(x) = x^{9/2}$, $x \geq 0$; $\left(\dfrac{f}{g}\right)(x) = \dfrac{1}{4}x^{1/2}$,

    $x \geq 0$; $(f \bullet g)(9) = 19{,}683$; $\left(\dfrac{f}{g}\right)(9) = \dfrac{3}{4}$

14. $-3 \leq x \leq 6$ and $x = 6$

Similarity: Equations and inequalities of this form take the same arithmetic procedure to solve.

Difference: For inequalities of this type, you must consider where the radicand is less than zero.

Answers

15. function 1: $y = a\sqrt{x-2} + k$, where a and k are real numbers

function 2: $y = a\sqrt{x-h} - 1$, where $a > 0$ and h is a real number

16. robin = 9.4 in., rabbit = 20.2 in.,
red squirrel = 14.5 in., hamster = 10.3 in.

17. a. $d = \dfrac{s^2}{200}$

b. 312.5 ft

Test B

1. -8 **2.** $9\sqrt{2}$ **3.** 3

4. $-2xyz^2\sqrt[3]{y^2z}$ **5.** 9

6. $-2 - 2\sqrt{2}$ **7.** $g(x) = \sqrt{x+3}$

8. $g(x) = 4\sqrt[3]{x}$ **9.** $g(x) = \sqrt[5]{x} + 1$

10. $g(x) = 3\sqrt{x} - 2$

11. Act 1 = 17.9 sec, Act 2 = 14.6 sec,
Act 3 = 23.1 sec, Act 4 = 40.0 sec

12. $(f + g)(x) = -3x^{2/5}$, all real numbers;
$(f - g)(x) = -x^{2/5}$, all real numbers;
$(f + g)(243) = -27$; $(f - g)(243) = -9$

13. $(f \bullet g)(x) = -\dfrac{8}{3}x^{5/2}$, $x \geq 0$; $\left(\dfrac{f}{g}\right)(x) = -\dfrac{1}{6}x^{1/2}$,
$x \geq 0$; $(f \bullet g)(4) = -\dfrac{256}{3}$; $\left(\dfrac{f}{g}\right)(4) = -\dfrac{1}{3}$

14. function 1: $y = a\sqrt{x+3} + k$, where a and k are real numbers

function 2: $y = a\sqrt{x-h} + 3$, where $a < 0$ and h is a real number

15. 5.60 ft (about 5 ft 7 in.)

16. $2 \leq x \leq 18$ and $x = 18$

Similarity: Equations and inequalities of this form take the same arithmetic procedure to solve.

Difference: For inequalities of this type, you must consider where the radicand is less than 0.

17. a. $p = (90m)^{1/3}$

b. 12,164 tennis rackets

Alternative Assessment

1. all expressions, a–f, equal 4

2. a. $A_1(x) = 6x^2$, $A_2(x) = x^2$

b. $A(x) = 6x^2 + 2x^2 = 8x^2$

c.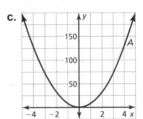

From the graph, the function fails the horizontal line test.

d. Restricting the domain to integers greater than or equal to zero will result in a function; This makes sense because there are no "negative" dimensions.

e. $x = \frac{1}{2}\sqrt{\frac{1}{2}A}$; The function solved for x represents one side of the diving platform in terms of the area of the whole dock.

f. The main landing will be $10 \times 15 = 150$ square feet, and each diving platform will be $5 \times 5 = 25$ square feet.

Chapter 6

6.1–6.4 Quiz

1. exponential growth; $1.75 > 1$

2. exponential decay; The power is negative with a base of $e > 1$.

3. $4e^4$ **4.** $27e^{6x}$ **5.** 5   **6.** $-9x$

7. $3^5 = 243$ **8.** $\log_2 0.125 = -3$

9. 1.544   **10.** 0.588   **11.** 4

12. 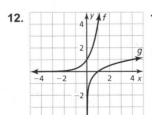   **13.**

Answers

14. $g(x) = \log_2 x + 3$ **15.** $g(x) = 4^{-x}$

16. $y = 8(1.05)^t$

Test A

1. 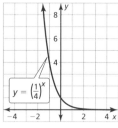   **2.**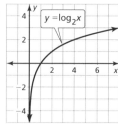

3.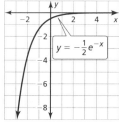

4. about 0.4854   **5.** about 5.1293

6. about 2.3219   **7.** about 2.8074

8. about 2.3219

9. reflection in the *x*-axis; $g(x) = -\log x$

10. reflection in the *y*-axis, followed by a horizontal shrink by a factor of $\frac{1}{2}$; $g(x) = e^{-2x}$

11. translation 2 units up; $g(x) = \frac{1}{2}^x + 2$

12. translation 3 units right and 1 unit up; $g(x) = e^{x-3} + 1$

13. All three expressions are equivalent by the Change-of-Base Formula.

14. $x = 3$ **15.** $x = 4$ **16.** $x = 1$

17. $x = 3$ **18.** 21 days

19. a. $18e^{0.231t}$

   b. exponential growth

   c. 181 million

20. $y = \frac{25}{2}(2^x)$, in about 8.32 years, so during 1998

Test B

1. 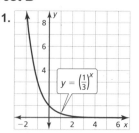   **2.**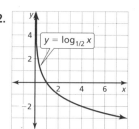

3.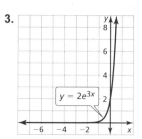

4. about 2.8907   **5.** about 0.5687

6. about 3.4594   **7.** about 1.7297

8. about 1.1610

9. translation 1 unit left; $g(x) = \log(x + 1)$

10. reflection in the *y*-axis; $g(x) = e^{-x}$

11. translation 2 units down; $g(x) = \frac{1}{2}^x - 2$

12. translation 2 units left and 3 units down; $g(x) = e^{x+2} - 3$

13. All three expressions are equivalent by the Change-of-Base Formula.

14. $x = 2$ **15.** $x = -1$ **16.** $x = 1$

17. $x = 8$ **18.** 8651 chain saws

19. a. $y = 1600e^{-0.23t}$

   b. exponential decay

   c. about 403 birds

20. $y = 20(3^x)$, about 6.29 years

Answers

Alternative Assessment

1. a. v_1 has an average finite difference of about 7, while v_2 has an average common ratio of about 1.2.

b. a linear model for v_1 and an exponential model for v_2

c. for v_1 : $v_1(t) = 3.4t + 353.2$,

for v_2 : $v_2(t) = 270.9(1.07)^t$

d. house 1: \$424,600, house 2: about \$1,121,678

e. about 43 years

f. during 2004; Graphically, look for the intersection of the two functions. Algebraically, set the functions equal and solve for t graphically because algebraically, it is generally impossible to isolate the variable t when equating a linear function to an exponential function. Numerical approximation is necessary.

g. The first house increases value at a constant rate, but more slowly than the second house. The second house increases more quickly over time; *Sample answer:* Many factors could affect value such as location, population growth, economic growth, or surrounding development.

Quarterly Standards Based Test

1. $p = -5$; To cancel the -2 in the last column, the product of 2 and $p + 6$ must be 2, so $p + 6 = 1$.

2. The leading coefficient is negative because both ends are down. The degree of the function is even because both ends go in the same direction. The degree is at least four because it has three turning points. It has two or four real zeros because non-real zeros come in pairs and there are only two obvious zeros. It is not clear what is happening around $x = 0$.

3. C

4. a. odd; $f(-x) = -f(x)$

b. neither; $f(-x) \neq -f(x)$; $f(-x) \neq f(x)$

c. even; $f(-x) = f(x)$

d. odd; $f(-x) = -f(x)$

e. even; $f(-x) = f(x)$

f. neither; $f(-x) \neq -f(x)$; $f(-x) \neq f(x)$

5. a. $g(x) = 1(x - 3)^2 + 4$

b. $g(x) = 1(x + 4)^2 - 3$

c. $g(x) = \frac{1}{3}(x - 0)^2 - 4$

d. $g(x) = 3(x + 2)^2 + 3$

6. B   **7.** D

8. $\sqrt[3]{b^2} = b^{4/6}$ because $\sqrt[3]{b^2} = (b^2)^{1/3} = b^{2/3} = b^{4/6}$. $b^{1/3} = \sqrt[3]{b}$ by the definition of rational exponents. $\sqrt[3]{b^3} = b$ because $\sqrt[3]{b^3} = (b^3)^{1/3} = b^{3/3} = b$.

9. $f(x) = |x + 2| + 3$

10. The degree is 3.

x	-2	-1	0	1	2	3	4	5
$f(x)$	-47	-17	-9	-11	-11	3	43	121

Finite differences are constant (12) at the third level, so the degree is 3; $f(x) = 2x^3 - 5x^2 + x - 9$

11. 17

12. $y = |x + 6|$, $y = x^2 - 7$; None have an inverse function.

Equation	Function	Has Inverse Function
$y = |x + 6|$	✓	
$x = (y - 1)^2$		
$y = x^2 - 7$	✓	
$x^2 = 4 - y^2$		

A function returns only one y-value for each x-value. Only functions have inverse functions, and neither of the functions passes the horizontal line test.

13. D

14. B; The leading coefficient is negative because the parabola opens down, and the y-intercept is 1.

15. yes; The graphs are symmetric about the line $y = x$.

16. $\frac{4}{3}, e^3, \sqrt{e}, 2.18$

Answers

17. no; *Sample answer:* An account that pays a higher interest rate may earn more interest if it pays a significantly higher interest rate. An account that pays a lower interest rate but pays compound interest more times per year may earn more interest.

18. a. $V(r) = \frac{4}{3}\pi r^3$

   b. $W(r) = \frac{4}{3}\pi(r-1)^3$

   c. *Sample answer:* $S(r) = \frac{4}{3}\pi\left[r^3 - (r-1)^3\right]$;

      $S(r) = V(r) - W(r)$

   d. $S(r) = 4\pi r^2 - 4\pi r + \frac{4}{3}\pi$; 1662.9 cm^3

19. A

20. The graph of g is a reflection in the x-axis and a translation 2 units left of the graph of f.

21. A, C, D, B

22. a. square root; $x = 7$ or $x = -3$; A perfect square equals a constant.

   b. complete the square; $x = 3 \pm \sqrt{2}$; The x-term is even.

   c. factoring method; $x = 4$ or $x = -5$; The trinomial is factorable.

   d. Quadratic Formula; $x = \pm\dfrac{\sqrt{10}}{2}i$; The other methods do not apply.

23.

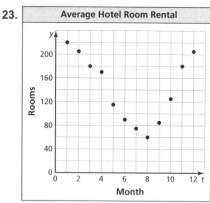

quadratic; $y = 4.53t^2 - 63.66t + 311.14$; It could have been either February or December.

Chapter 7

7.1–7.2 Quiz

1. neither; The products and quotients of x and y are not constant.

2. direct variation; The quotients of x and y are constant.

3. inverse variation; The products of x and y are constant.

4. neither; The products and quotients of x and y are not constant.

5. direct variation; The quotients of x and y are constant.

6. $y = \dfrac{16}{x}$; $y = -4$

7. C   **8.** B   **9.** A

10. $g(x) = \dfrac{6}{x+3} + 2$; translation 3 units left and 2 units up

11.

Leaking rate (gal/min)	Time (min)
6	15
8	11.25
18	5
24	3.75
30	3

Test A

1. $y = \dfrac{14}{x}$, $y = -7$ **2.** $y = -\dfrac{39}{x}$, $y = \dfrac{39}{2}$

3. $y = -\dfrac{30}{x}$, $y = 15$ **4.** $y = \dfrac{4}{x}$, $y = -2$

5. h is negative. k is negative.

6. h is positive. k is positive.

7. $h = 0$; k is negative.

8. h is negative. k is negative.

9. $\dfrac{2y^3}{7x}$ **10.** $\dfrac{x^2 + 5x}{x + 2}$

11. $\dfrac{x^2 - 7x - 22}{x^2 + 9x + 14}$ **12.** $\dfrac{x - 5}{x + 3}$

Answers

13. $\dfrac{h^2}{2j^2}$

14. $\dfrac{x-1}{x^2-4}$

15. 2308 muffins

16. two more families

17. $y = x - 8$, $x \neq -2$; yes; They will look different

because $f(x) = \dfrac{(x-8)(x+2)}{(x+2)}$ is undefined at

$x = -2$.

18. a. $V = 40r^3$; $r = \dfrac{1}{2}\sqrt[3]{\dfrac{V}{5}}$ b. about 52.3%

19. about 54.55 mi/h

Test B

1. $y = -\dfrac{29}{x}$, $y = -\dfrac{29}{2}$ 2. $y = \dfrac{88}{x}$, $y = 44$

3. $y = \dfrac{36}{x}$, $y = 18$ 4. $y = \dfrac{1}{2x}$, $y = \dfrac{1}{4}$

5. h is positive. k is positive.

6. h is positive; $k = 0$

7. h is negative. k is positive.

8. $h = 0$; k is positive.

9. $\dfrac{10b}{a^2}$ 10. $\dfrac{t+1}{t+4}$ 11. $\dfrac{x-4}{x+4}$

12. $\dfrac{p^2+5p}{p+6}$ 13. $\dfrac{28n}{15m^2}$ 14. $\dfrac{4m-31}{m^2-64}$

15. 1366 heart-shaped chocolate-covered strawberries

16. 400 cycles per second

17. $y = x - 3$, $x \neq 4$; yes; They will look different

because $f(x) = \dfrac{(x-3)(x-4)}{(x-4)}$ is undefined at

$x = 4$.

18. a. $V = 128r^3$; $r = \dfrac{1}{4}\sqrt[3]{\dfrac{V}{2}}$ b. about 47.64%

19. 2.5 mL

Alternative Assessment

1. a. *Sample answer:*

$$f(x) = \dfrac{(x+3)(x-2)(x+1)}{(x+1)} = x^2 + x - 6$$

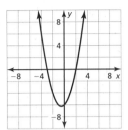

In general, answers should contain the factors $(x+3)$ and $(x-2)$ in the numerator, and have no variable in the denominator after simplification, such as $f(x) = x^2 + x - 6$.

b. *Sample answer:* $f(x) = \dfrac{(x+3)(x-2)(x+1)}{(x-1)}$

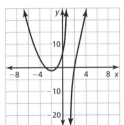

In general, answers should contain the factors $(x+3)$ and $(x-2)$ in the numerator, and the factor $(x-1)$ in the denominator after simplification. The degree of the numerator must be larger than the degree of the denominator to ensure no horizontal asymptotes.

c. *Sample answer:* $f(x) = \dfrac{2(x+3)(x-2)}{(x-1)^2}$

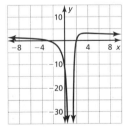

Answers should contain the factors $(x+3)$ and $(x-2)$ in the numerator, and the factor $(x-1)$ in the denominator. The degree of the numerator must be equal to the degree of the denominator, and the ratio of the leading coefficients of the numerator to the denominator must be 2.

Answers

2. a. $h = \dfrac{21.7}{\pi r^2}$

b. $S = 2\pi r^2 + \dfrac{43.4}{r}$

c. $S = \dfrac{2\pi r^3 + 43.4}{r}$; no; because the degree of the numerator is greater than the degree of the denominator

d. minimum ≈ 43.1 in.^{2}, $r \approx 1.5$ in., $h \approx 3.03$ in.

e. The actual can is taller and has a smaller diameter.

f. *Sample answer:* A smaller diameter might be easier to hold, especially for younger people.

Chapter 8

8.1–8.3 Quiz

1. 30, $a_n = 7n - 5$

2. -15, $a_n = (-1)^n \cdot 3n$

3. $\dfrac{5}{25}$, $a_n = \dfrac{n}{5n}$

4. $\displaystyle\sum_{i=1}^{12} i$, 78

5. $\displaystyle\sum_{i=1}^{7} \dfrac{1}{2i}$, $\dfrac{363}{280}$

6. $a_n = 2n$

7. $a_n = n - 3$

8. arithmetic, $a_n = 4n - 24$, 12

9. neither, $a_n = \dfrac{n+1}{n+2}$, $\dfrac{10}{11}$

10. geometric, $a_n = -1(-4)^{n-1}$, $-65{,}536$

11. $a_n = 4n - 11$

12. 35

13. -189

14. a. $152.44

b. $20.61

Test A

1. 28

2. 4092

3. 2

4. 55

5. 6175

6. $\dfrac{50}{13}$

7. neither

8. arithmetic; $a_n = 4n + 3$

9. geometric; $a_n = 2 \cdot (2)^{n-1}$

10. arithmetic; $a_n = 2n - 2$

11. $a_1 = -3$, $a_n = -2a_{n-1}$, $a_7 = -192$

12. $a_1 = 8$, $a_n = a_{n-1} + 4$; $a_7 = 32$

13. $a_1 = 16$, $a_n = \frac{1}{4}a_{n-1}$; $a_7 = \dfrac{1}{256}$

14. $a_1 = -2$, $a_n = a_{n-1} - 3$; $a_7 = -20$

15. $a_1 = 5$, $a_n = a_{n-1} - 3$; $a_n = -3n + 8$

16. a. n represents the number of rows, a_n represents the total number of cans in row n

b.

n	a_n
1	1
2	4
3	9
4	16
5	25
6	36
7	49
8	64

c. $a_n = n^2$

17. a. $625 **b.** $7750

18. a. 6.328 in. **b.** 65.762 in.

Test B

1. 4753

2. 20

3. $\dfrac{15}{2}$

4. $\dfrac{5456}{3}$

5. 36

6. 2

7. arithmetic; $a_n = -6n + 6$

8. neither; $a_1 = 4$, $a_2 = 3$, $a_n = a_{n-2} + a_{n-1}$

9. geometric; $a_n = \frac{1}{2} \cdot (3)^{n-1}$

10. geometric; $a_n = 4 \cdot \left(\frac{1}{2}\right)^{n-1}$

11. $a_1 = -2$, $a_n = a_{n-1} - 5$; $a_6 = -27$

12. $a_1 = 125$, $a_n = \frac{1}{5}a_{n-1}$; $a_6 = \dfrac{1}{25}$

13. $a_1 = 1$, $a_n = a_{n-1} - 2$; $a_6 = -9$

Answers

14. $a_1 = 2,\ a_n = 4a_{n-1} + 1;\ a_6 = 2379$

15. $a_1 = 3,\ a_n = -3a_{n-1};\ a_n = -3(-3)^{n-1}$

16. a. n represents the number of rows, and a_n represents the total number of oranges in row n

b.

n	a_n
1	1
2	3
3	6
4	10
5	15
6	21
7	28
8	36

c. $a_n = \dfrac{n(n+1)}{2}$

17. a. $a_n = 3320 + 180n$ **b.** \$5480

18. after June's savings

19. a. 4.096 in. **b.** 31.611 in.

Alternative Assessment

1. a. arithmetic; There is a constant difference of \$50 between each game.

b. \$100

c. $a_n = 50 + 50n$

d. \$1300

2. a. geometric; The number of ancestors doubles with each generation.

b. $a_n = 2^{n-1}$

c. 8

d. current year $- 240$

e. 4095

Chapter 9

9.1–9.4 Quiz

1. $\cos\theta = \dfrac{\sqrt{65}}{9},\ \tan\theta = \dfrac{4}{\sqrt{65}},\ \csc\theta = \dfrac{9}{4},$

$\sec\theta = \dfrac{9}{\sqrt{65}},\ \cot\theta = \dfrac{\sqrt{65}}{4}$

2. $x = 10\sqrt{2}$ **3.** $x = 5\sqrt{3}$

4. *Sample answer:* $410°$ and $-310°$

5. *Sample answer:* $\dfrac{13\pi}{4}$ and $\dfrac{-3\pi}{4}$

6. *Sample answer:* $80°$ and $-280°$

7. $157.5°$ **8.** $\dfrac{-4\pi}{9}$ **9.** $\dfrac{16\pi}{45}$

10. $\sin\theta = -\dfrac{6}{\sqrt{40}},\ \cos\theta = -\dfrac{2}{\sqrt{40}},\ \tan\theta = 3,$

$\csc\theta = -\dfrac{\sqrt{40}}{6},\ \sec\theta = -\dfrac{\sqrt{40}}{2},\ \cot\theta = \dfrac{1}{3}$

11. $\sin\theta = 0,\ \cos\theta = -1,\ \tan\theta = 0,$
$\csc\theta = $ undefined, $\sec\theta = -1,$
$\cot\theta = $ undefined

12. amplitude: $a = 5$, period: $\dfrac{2\pi}{b} = \dfrac{2\pi}{1} = 2\pi;$
vertical stretch by factor of 5

13. You travel $1250\pi \approx 3927$ feet; Your friend travels $850\pi \approx 2670$ feet.

Test A

1.

$$\dfrac{(\sin x + \cos x)^2}{1 + 2\sin x\cos x} = \dfrac{\sin^2 x + 2\sin x\cos x + \cos^2 x}{1 + 2\sin x\cos x}$$

$$= \dfrac{\sin^2 x + \cos^2 x + \sin x\cos x}{1 + 2\sin x\cos x}$$

$$= \dfrac{1 + 2\sin x\cos x}{1 + 2\sin x\cos x}$$

$$= 1$$

2. $\sin\left(x + \dfrac{\pi}{2}\right) = \sin x \bullet \cos\dfrac{\pi}{2} + \cos x \bullet \sin\dfrac{\pi}{2}$

$= \sin x \bullet 0 + \cos x \bullet 1$

$= \cos x$

Answers

3. $\dfrac{\sin x - \cos x}{\sin x} + \dfrac{\cos x - \sin x}{\cos x}$

$= \dfrac{(\sin x - \cos x)\cos x}{\sin x \cos x} + \dfrac{(\cos x - \sin x)}{\sin x \cos x}$

$= \dfrac{\sin x \cos x - \cos^2 x}{\sin x \cos x} + \dfrac{\sin x \cos x - \sin^2 x}{\sin x \cos x}$

$= \dfrac{2 \sin x \cos x - \sin^2 x - \cos^2 x}{\sin x \cos x}$

$= \dfrac{2 \sin x \cos x - \left(\sin^2 x + \cos^2 x\right)}{\sin x \cos x}$

$= \dfrac{2 \sin x \cos x - 1}{\sin x \cos x}$

$= \dfrac{2 \sin x \cos x}{\sin x \cos x} - \dfrac{1}{\sin x \cos x}$

$= 2 - \dfrac{1}{\sin x} \cdot \dfrac{1}{\cos x}$

$= 2 - \csc x \sec x$

$= 2 - \sec x \csc x$

4. 2   5. 1   6. $-\dfrac{2\sqrt{3}}{3}$

7. $y = 4 \sin x$ 8. $y = 4 \sin\left(x + \dfrac{\pi}{2}\right)$

9. $y = -2 \cos \frac{1}{2}x$ 10. $y = 2 \cos \frac{1}{2}x + 2$

11.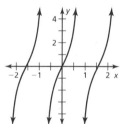

vertical stretch by a factor of 2 and a horizontal shrink by a factor of $\frac{1}{2}$

12.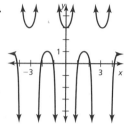

horizontal shrink by a factor of $\frac{1}{2}$, followed by a translation 2 units up

13. $128.57°$; *Sample answer:* $\dfrac{19\pi}{7} \approx 488.57°$ and $-\dfrac{9\pi}{7} \approx -231.43°$

14. $-\dfrac{13\pi}{18}$; *Sample answer:* $230° = \dfrac{23\pi}{18}$ and $-490° = \dfrac{49\pi}{18}$

15. $585°$; *Sample answer:* $\dfrac{5\pi}{4} = 225°$ and $-\dfrac{3\pi}{4} = -135°$

16. arc length $= 10\pi \approx 31.42$ in.; area $= 300\pi = 942.48$ in.^{2}

17. $-\sqrt{10}$ 18. $\dfrac{\sqrt{10}}{3}$ 19. -3

20. $\dfrac{-\sqrt{10}}{\sqrt{10}}$ 21. $\dfrac{3\sqrt{10}}{10}$ 22. $-\frac{1}{3}$

23. Quadrant IV   24. 232 ft

Test B

1. $\sin^2 x + \sin^2 x \cot^2 x = \sin^2 x\left(1 + \cot^2 x\right)$

$= \sin^2 x\left(\csc^2 x\right)$

$= \sin^2 x\left(\dfrac{1}{\sin^2 x}\right)$

$= 1$

Answers

2. $1 - \dfrac{\cos^2 x}{1 + \sin x} = \dfrac{1(1 + \sin x)}{1 + \sin x} - \dfrac{\cos^2 x}{1 + \sin x}$

$\qquad\qquad\qquad = \dfrac{1 + \sin x - \cos^2 x}{1 + \sin x}$

$\qquad\qquad\qquad = \dfrac{1 - \cos^2 x + \sin x}{1 + \sin x}$

$\qquad\qquad\qquad = \dfrac{\sin^2 x + \sin x}{1 + \sin x}$

$\qquad\qquad\qquad = \dfrac{\sin x(\sin x + 1)}{1 + \sin x}$

$\qquad\qquad\qquad = \dfrac{\sin x(1 + \sin x)}{1 + \sin x}$

$\qquad\qquad\qquad = \sin x$

3. $\cos\left(x - \dfrac{5\pi}{6}\right) = \cos x \bullet \cos \dfrac{5\pi}{6} + \sin x \bullet \sin \dfrac{5\pi}{6}$

$\qquad\qquad\qquad = \cos x \bullet -\dfrac{\sqrt{3}}{2} + \sin x \bullet \dfrac{1}{2}$

$\qquad\qquad\qquad = -\dfrac{\sqrt{3}}{2}\cos x + \dfrac{1}{2}\sin x$

4. $\dfrac{-2\sqrt{3}}{3}$ **5.** -1 **6.** -2

7. $y = -5\cos x$ **8.** $y = \frac{1}{2}\cos(2x - 2\pi)$

9. $y = -2\sin 2x$ **10.** $y = 4\sin(2\pi x) + 3$

11.

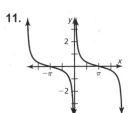

vertical shrink by a factor of $\frac{1}{2}$, and a horizontal stretch by a factor of 2

12.

horizontal shrink by a factor of $\dfrac{1}{2\pi}$

13. $-\dfrac{28\pi}{9}$; *Sample answer:* $160° = \dfrac{8\pi}{9}$ and

$\qquad -200° = -\dfrac{10\pi}{9}$

14. $108°$; *Sample answer:* $\dfrac{13\pi}{5} = 468°$ and

$\qquad -\dfrac{7\pi}{5} = -252°$

15. $\dfrac{17\pi}{18}$; *Sample answer:* $530° = -\dfrac{53\pi}{18}$ and

$\qquad -190° = -\dfrac{19\pi}{18}$

16. arc length $= \dfrac{35\pi}{9} = 12.22$ in.;

$\qquad$ area $= \dfrac{175\pi}{9} = 61.09$ in.^{2}

17. $-\frac{5}{3}$ **18.** $-\frac{5}{4}$ **19.** $\frac{4}{3}$

20. $-\frac{3}{5}$ **21.** $-\frac{4}{5}$ **22.** $\frac{3}{4}$

23. Quadrant III

24. $y = 20\sin\left(\dfrac{\pi}{5}x + \dfrac{3\pi}{2}\right) + 25$

Alternative Assessment

1. a. $\sin\theta = -\frac{2}{3}$

   b. $\csc\theta = -\frac{3}{2}$

   c. $\cos\theta = -\dfrac{\sqrt{5}}{3}$

   d. $\sec\theta = -\dfrac{3\sqrt{5}}{5}$

   e. $\cot\theta = \dfrac{\sqrt{5}}{2}$

Answers

2. a.

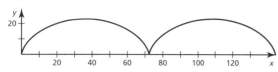

yes; This is a periodic function as the values repeat exactly and continuously as the wheel rotates through $360°$ turns.

b. 13 in.

c. 24.5 in.

d. about 23 in.

Quarterly Standards Based Test

1. B and D; The vertex is at $(4, 12)$ and the graph opens down; $-3(x - 4)^2 + 12 = -3x^2 + 24x - 36$

2. 12, 4, and -8; $y = \dfrac{12x + 9}{4x - 8}$

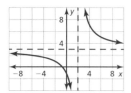

3. a. Loan #1 is represented by a linear function and Loan #2 is represented by an exponential function.

b. The amounts in Loan #1 are decreasing by the constant amount $450 each year. So, the function is linear. The amounts in Loan #2 are decreasing by the constant ratio 0.96 each year. So, the function is exponential.

c. After 10 years, the balance of Loan #1 ($9950) is greater than the balance of Loan #2 ($9695.30). After 15 years, the balance of Loan #2 ($7905.20) is greater than the balance of Loan #1 ($7700.00).

4. 8, $64^{1/2} = 8$, $64^{2/3} = 16$, $8^{4/3} = 16$,

$(\sqrt[3]{64})^3 = 64$, $(\sqrt{64})^3 = 512$

5. $D = \dfrac{215x - 134.2}{(x + 1.6)(1.2x + 9)} = \dfrac{215x - 134.2}{1.2x^2 + 10.92x + 14.4}$

6. D; $q = \dfrac{120}{p + r}$

7. 12 games; $\dfrac{6 \times 158 + 12 \times 170}{18} = 166$

8. B

9. a. $a_n = 1.00375a_{n-1} - 200$

b. $6789.45

c. 50 months

d. 32 months; Total of payments at $200 per month is $9875.59. Total of payments at $300 per month is $9564.70. The amount saved is $310.89.

10. The average rates of change from least to greatest are B (0.4), A (0.79), C (0.85), and D (1).

11. *Sample answer:* $F = 1210(0.76)^x$ (Numbers may vary due to roundoff because table values are not exact.); The relationship is exponential decay.

12.

Function	Positive real zeros	Negative real zeros	Imaginary zeros	Total zeros
$f(x)$	3	2	2	7
$g(x)$	1	2	0	3
$h(x)$	4	1	4	9

$f(x)$ has a maximum of four sign changes, because there are five real zeros; $g(x)$ has a maximum of two sign changes, because there are three real zeros; $h(x)$ has a maximum of four sign changes, because there are five real zeros.

13. a. two pure imaginary solutions; $x = \pm 5i$

b. two real number solutions; $x = \pm\sqrt{14}$

c. two real number solutions; $x = 1$, $x = 4$

d. one pure imaginary solution; $x = 3i$

e. one imaginary solution; $x = -2 + 11i$

f. two imaginary solution; $x = \dfrac{-1 \pm i\sqrt{31}}{2}$

g. one real solution; $x = -3$

h. two real solutions; $x = \dfrac{-3 \pm \sqrt{29}}{2}$

14. $\cot x \sec x \sin x$; $\sec^2 x - \tan^2 x$; $\dfrac{\sin\left(\dfrac{\pi}{2} - x\right)}{\cos x}$

Answers

15. B

16. a. $y_1 = 1.3 \sin(0.5x - 0.44) + 3.1;$
$\qquad y_2 = 1.3 \sin(0.5x - 0.06) + 3.1$

b.

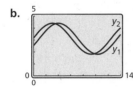

The graph of y_1 is a horizontal translation 1 unit right of the graph of y_2.

c. The dock that is closest to the mouth of the inlet will reach high tide before a dock that is farther away. Because Dock #2 reaches its maximum height earlier, it is closest to the mouth of the inlet.

17. a. 2

b. 2.096

c. 3

d. 2.93

e. 0.834

f. 0

$\log_3 1, \log_3 \frac{5}{2}, \log 100, \log_3 10, \log_3 25, \ln e^3$

18. C

19. a. $\theta < 5$ radians

b. $\cos \theta < 0$

c. $\theta > 45°$

20. $x = -1, x = 2, x = \frac{4}{3}$

Chapter 10

10.1–10.3 Quiz

1. $\frac{3}{5}$ **2.** 0.47   **3.** $\frac{3}{7}$

4. 0.98   **5.** $\frac{1}{6}, \frac{6}{25}$ **6.** $0.2\overline{6}$

7. 0.175

8. a. 0.0156

b. 0.96

c. 0.0286

9. probability that the person chooses the first benefit package = 0.45; probability that the person chooses the second benefit package = 0.55; probability that the person is a man = 0.4; probability that the person is a woman = 0.6

Test A

1. $\frac{1}{6}$ **2.** $\frac{1}{2}$ **3.** $\frac{1}{2}$

4. 0   **5.** 10   **6.** 210

7. 70   **8.** 1680   **9.** Company 1

10. no; If A and B were independent events, then $P(A) \cdot P(B) = \frac{3}{14} \cdot \frac{1}{5} = \frac{3}{70}$, not $\frac{3}{65}$.

11. $160x^3 y^3$ **12.** $-108{,}864x^5 y^3$

13. a. about 50.27%

b. about 49.73%

c. about 12.7%

14. a.

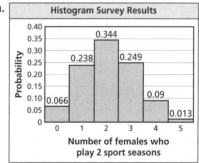

b. 2 of the 5 female students will play 2 sport seasons

c. about 35.2%

15. a. $\frac{7}{13}$ **b.** $\frac{12}{221}$

16. a. $\frac{1}{455}$ **b.** $\frac{1}{2730}$

Test B

1. $\frac{1}{8}$ **2.** $\frac{3}{8}$ **3.** $\frac{1}{2}$

4. 0   **5.** 95,040   **6.** 35

7. 1716   **8.** 3024   **9.** Book Class

Answers

10. yes; Switching the event names A and B in the text formula $P(A \text{ and } B) = P(A) \bullet P(B \mid A)$ gives the formula $P(B \text{ and } A) = P(B) \bullet P(A \mid B)$. But $P(B \text{ and } A) = P(A \text{ and } B)$, so the given formula is in fact equivalent to the formula stated in the text.

11. $2{,}520{,}000y^5$ 12. $26{,}730x^7y^8$

13. **a.** 10%
   b. 90%
   c. 0.1%

14. **a.**

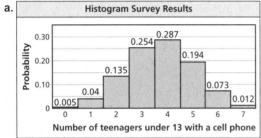

b. 4 teenagers under the age of 13 will own a cell phone

c. about 56.6%

15. **a.** $\frac{5}{21}$

  b. $\frac{10}{147}$

  c. $\frac{1}{21}$

16. **a.** $\frac{1}{1140}$

  b. $\frac{1}{6840}$

Alternative Assessment

1. **a.** odd; *Sample answer:* There are 5 odd spaces and 4 even. The probability of landing on an odd is $\frac{5}{9}$ and the probability of landing on an even is $\frac{4}{9}$. But this does not mean you are more likely to win the game because the game is based on the product of two spins, not just one spin.

  b. independent; The second spin is not affected by the first.

  c. There are 81 possible outcomes.

d. (1, 1), (1, 2), (1, 3), (1, 4), (1, 5), (1, 6), (1, 7), (1, 8), (1, 9), (2, 1), (2, 2), (2, 3), (2, 4), (2, 5), (2, 6), (2, 7) (2, 8), (2, 9), (3, 1), (3, 2), (3, 3), (3, 4), (3, 5), (3, 6), (3, 7), (3, 8), (3, 9), (4, 1), (4, 2), (4, 3), (4, 4), (4, 5), (4, 6), (4, 7), (4, 8), (4, 9), (5, 1), (5, 2), (5, 3), (5, 4), (5, 5), (5, 6), (5, 7), (5, 8), (5, 9), (6, 1), (6, 2), (6, 3), (6, 4), (6, 5), (6, 6), (6, 7), (6, 8), (6, 9), (7, 1), (7, 2), (7, 3), (7, 4), (7, 5), (7, 6), (7, 7), (7, 8), (7, 9), (8, 1), (8, 2), (8, 3), (8, 4), (8, 5), (8, 6), (8, 7), (8, 8), (8, 9), (9, 1), (9, 2), (9, 3), (9, 4) (9, 5), (9, 6), (9, 7), (9, 8), (9, 9)

e. $\frac{25}{81}$

f. $\frac{56}{81}$

g. no; *Sample answer:* You lose if the product of the two numbers is even, and you are more than twice as likely to have an even product than an odd product.

h. One spin must be a prime number and the other must be 1.

i. *Sample answer:* The probability of the first described turn is $\frac{1}{9} \bullet \frac{5}{9} = \frac{5}{81}$. So, $P(\text{Turn 1}) = \frac{5}{81}$; The probability of the second described turn is $\frac{5}{9} \bullet \frac{1}{9} = \frac{5}{81}$. So, $P(\text{Turn 2}) = \frac{5}{81}$. Then $P(\text{Turn 1 or Turn 2}) = \frac{5}{81} + \frac{5}{81} = \frac{10}{81}$.

j. *Sample answer:* Because there are an odd number of possible outcomes, the game cannot be made perfectly fair. But by changing the operation to addition of the two integers, the probability of an even sum is $\frac{41}{81} \approx 0.506$.

k. *Sample answer:* You could make it less likely to spin an even product by making the area of the even triangles smaller than the odd.

Chapter 11

11.1–11.3 Quiz

1. 0.8944   2. 0.0659   3. 0.1908

4. no   5. yes

Answers

6. population: college students, sample: 1423 college students surveyed

7. parameter   **8.** experiment

9. a. self-selected sample

   b. yes; Self-selection may tend toward more extreme reviews.

   c. *Sample answer:* Require every tenth customer to fill out the survey.

10. The survey question is biased; "Prize-winning coffee" influences the person being asked.

Test A

1. experiment

2. a. convenience sample

   b. biased

3. self-selected sample   **4.** parameters

5. a. The patients are divided into groups based on high/low number of blood clots. The medication may have more of an effect on one group than the other.

   b. Randomly assign the patients to the treatment and control groups. (Randomly mix high/low blood-clot patients.)

6. 81.5%   **7.** 84%   **8.** 16%

9. 84%   **10.** 2.5%

11. a. $\overline{X}_{control}$ = 1.103 g/mL, $\overline{X}_{treatment}$ = 1.166 g/mL

   b. 0.063 g/mL

   c.

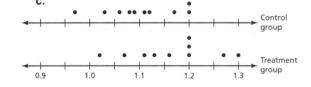

12. a. population: all U.S. teenagers, sample: 2200 randomly selected U.S. teenagers surveyed

   b. ±1.16%

   c. 90.84%–93.16%

   d. the survey with 2200 U.S. teenagers; The smaller survey has a smaller sample size and a larger margin of error, and the results are based on a convenience sample.

Test B

1. observational study

2. a. simple random sample

   b. unbiased

3. stratified sample   **4.** statistics

5. a. The sample size is not large enough to produce valid results.

   b. To improve the validity, the sample size must be larger and the experiment must be replicated.

6. 84%   **7.** 16%   **8.** 2.5%

9. 81.5%   **10.** 84%

11. a. $\overline{X}_{control}$ ≈ 13.04 cm, $\overline{X}_{treatment}$ = 17.17 cm

   b. 4.12 cm

   c.

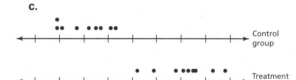

12. a. population: all U.S. drivers, sample: 3500 randomly selected U.S. drivers surveyed

   b. ±1.64%

   c. 60.36%–63.64%

   d. the survey with 3500 U.S. drivers; The smaller survey has a smaller sample size and a larger margin of error, and the results are based on a convenience sample.

Answers

Alternative Assessment

1. a. systematic sample; The sample is biased; All grade levels attend the first lunch, but mainly juniors and seniors will be affected by the decision.

b. stratified sample; This sample is relatively unbiased; A random selection of juniors and seniors are surveyed, but some may not be planning on attending the prom so they have no stake in the outcome.

c. The student council could use any process in which students are separated into classes (such as English, 9, 10, 11, and 12) or groups, and then a set of those classes (or groups) is randomly selected to survey every student in the class (or group).

d. 108; with a margin of error of about $\pm 10\%$; no

e. $\pm 10\%$; no

f. no; A margin of error of $\pm 2\%$ requires a sample size of 2500. One quarter of the student body is 435 students. The least margin of error possible for a survey of that size is $\pm 5\%$.

g. no; Because the margin of error is about $\pm 4.78\%$, the exact percent of the students wanting to keep the prom in its current location is between about 41.22% and 50.78%. Similarly, the percentage of students wanting to change the venue is between about 49.22% and 58.78%. The overlap in the intervals makes it impossible to determine for sure the desires of the students.

Quarterly Standards Based Test

1. a.

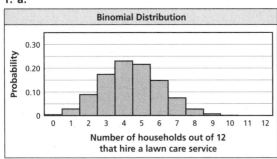

b. 4 households

c. $P(k \leq 6) \approx 0.89$

2. $\theta_1, \theta_3, \theta_4, \theta_5, \theta_2, \theta_6$; The values $\cos \theta$ decrease over the interval $\left[0, \dfrac{\pi}{2}\right]$.

3. 2100 different pizzas   **4.** C, F

5. There are a total of 16 elements in the diagram and 5 of those elements are in both A and B. So, $P(A \text{ and } B) = \frac{5}{16}$. There are a total of 16 elements in the diagram and 5 of those elements are in B. So, $P(B) = \frac{5}{16}$. So, in this diagram, $P(A \text{ and } B) = P(B)$.

6. a. The sequence has a geometric pattern and each term is the previous term multiplied by -5.

b. $\dfrac{625}{2}$

c.

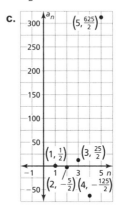

d. $a_1 = \frac{1}{2}$; $a_n = -5a_{n-1}$

7. a.

		Class		
		Sign Language	French	Total
Gender	Female	33	19	52
	Male	21	22	43
	Total	54	41	95

b. $P(\text{male and French}) = \frac{22}{95} \approx 0.232$

c. $P(\text{sign language given Female}) = \frac{33}{52} \approx 0.635$

8. $y < -x^2 - 2x + 3$
$y \geq x^2 + 2x - 8$

Answers

9. a. $x + y + z = -1$

$\quad 2x + y + 2z = 1$

$\quad 5x - y + 5z = 13$

b. $x + y + z = -1$

$\quad x - y + z = 4$

$\quad 5x - y + 5z = 13$

10. a. biased; The board members select homes that are readily available. So, the sample is a convenience sample. The sample is biased because other homes do not have an opportunity to be chosen.

b. biased; The students can choose whether or not to participate. So, the sample is a self-selected sample. The sample is biased because students who fill out the survey most likely have a strong opinion on the subject of food selections.

c. biased; Most of the patrons of a skateboard park are typically under the age of 20. So, the sample is surveying individuals who are not in their target population. The sample is biased because the majority of the patrons do not have an opportunity to fill out the survey.

d. This survey is unbiased.

11. all students: parameter, 300 students: statistic; The standard deviation for all students is a parameter because it is a characteristic of the population. The standard deviation for the 300 students is a statistic because it is a characteristic of the sample.

12. a. 560 students

b. Only 17% of the students prefer kettle corn. Approximately three times as many students prefer buttered popcorn.

c. 3.25%

d. Six is a small sample size and it is possible for five of them to prefer kettle corn.

e. 40.8%

13.

Equation	Is the inverse a function?		Is the equation its own inverse?	
	Yes	No	Yes	No
$y = 2^x - 3$	X			X
$y = 5 - x$	X		X	
$y = \dfrac{3}{x}$	X		X	
$y = x^2 + 4$		X		X

14. a. 77.45%

b. between 39 and 54

15. B and C

Post Course Test

1. $g(x) = -3x + 3$

2. $g(x) = \frac{1}{3}(x + 2)^2$

3. $g(x) = \sqrt{-\frac{1}{5}x}$

4. $g(x) = e^{x-2} - 3$

5. $c = 0.25t + 9$

6. $x = 5, y = 1, z = -2$

7. $66\frac{2}{3}$ megabytes

8. a. 0.25 sec

b. 4 ft

9.

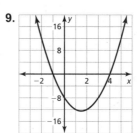

10. $(y + 2)^2 = 4x$

11. $y = \frac{1}{3}(x - 3)^2 - 1$

12. $y = x^2 + 2x + 2$

13. *Sample answer:* $y = x^3 - 5x^2 + x - 5$; Any equation of the form $y = a(x - 5)(x^2 + 1)$ will meet the description.

14. $x = -3, x = -4$

15. $x = 2 \pm 2i$

16. $x = \pm 2, x = \pm 2i$

17. $x = 12$

18. $x = -\frac{2}{9}, x = 0$

19. $x = 113$

20. $y = 100(1.5)^x$

21. \$209.92

22. $\dfrac{\sqrt{2}}{2}$

23. $2(x + 2)$

24. $\pm i\dfrac{\sqrt{2}}{2}$ and $-\dfrac{1}{2}$

25. $\log_2 \frac{1}{9}$

26. $x \neq 2$

Answers

27.

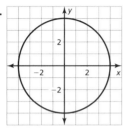

28. $\dfrac{x + 1}{x - 1}$

29. $-\dfrac{8x + 9}{x^2 + x - 6}$

30. 57

31. $\dfrac{9}{4}$

32. $\dfrac{43}{45}\pi$

33. 300°

34. $\dfrac{\sqrt{3}}{2}$

35.

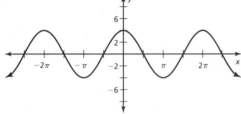

36. $y = 2 \cos x$

37. $-\tan \theta$

38. $\dfrac{\sqrt{3} - 1}{2\sqrt{2}} = \dfrac{\sqrt{2}\left(\sqrt{3} - 1\right)}{4}$

39. 0.65

40. 2,598,960 ways

41. 0.2757

42. 0.815

43. The population is the entire student body. The sample is the set of eight randomly selected students, two students selected from each grade.

44. systematic random sampling method

45. The interval 0.265 to 0.275 is likely to contain the exact percentage of students.

46. 0.22

47. observational study